# PRACTICAL STAINED GLASS CRAFT

Janet (see page 161)

# PRACTICAL
# STAINED GLASS CRAFT

Jo Frohbieter-Mueller

**David & Charles**
Newton Abbot   London

**Hippocrene Books Inc**
New York

I gratefully acknowledge the help of Dr Wayne Mueller
for his support and suggestions during the preparation of the manuscript.

Thanks also to Tudor Summers and Paul San
Casciani AMGP, for their expert advice.

**British Library Cataloguing in Publication Data**
Frohbieter-Mueller, Jo
Practical stained glass craft.
1. Glass painting and staining—Techniques
I. Title
748.5′028    TT298

ISBN 0–7153–8516–X (Great Britain)
ISBN 0–88254–888–3 (United States)

Phototypeset by ABM Typographics Ltd, Hull
and text printed in Great Britain
by Butler & Tanner Ltd Frome
for David & Charles (Publishers) Limited
Brunel House   Newton Abbot   Devon

# Contents

To my children, Janet and D. Tom
who see the world through rose-coloured windows

# Introduction

Stained glass is attracting increasing numbers of people who not only enjoy the beauty of the glass but also enjoy working and creating with it. To the uninitiated the techniques may look difficult, but they are quite the opposite. Tools have been developed in recent years that make working with stained glass a joy, and the exquisite glass now being produced entices even the most hesitant individuals into the field. Stained-glass art objects are often prohibitively expensive to buy; when you learn to make them yourself you can transform your home into a spectrum of colours, delight your family and friends with lovely gifts, or even develop a cottage industry.

**Getting Started**
But what can you do with glass when you first begin to work with it? You are a novice for only a short time, because the techniques are readily acquired, and then you must look for ways to ply your skills.

This book offers you a collection of different types of stained-glass projects, each one being graded for difficulty: those rated 1 are the easiest to make, those rated 10 the most advanced. The cartoons (patterns) for many of them are drawn full-size and those that are not can easily be enlarged, using the method described on page 39. Most of the projects can be either foiled or leaded. The necessary techniques and procedures are explained and illustrated in full.

# 1   The Uses of Stained Glass

Stained glass has been used for centuries to motivate worshippers, as a source of inspiration and education in churches and cathedrals, and is extensively used in schools, colleges and public buildings. Its use in domestic dwellings is much more recent, but the rush to buy and display it in today's homes suggests an effort to make up for lost time.

Domestic stained glass has been used in windows in place of clear panes where natural sunlight plays upon the glass, changing the images and colours as the sun crosses the sky. But the use of coloured glass is not limited to exterior windows. The following pages will explain how it can be used throughout the home as a powerful decorating tool that establishes moods and is a source of beauty.

## Doors

The first impression one gets of a home is determined by the door. It can be a plain wooden door or it can be a burst of light! Doors are excellent locations for stained glass. Interestingly, a design does not lose its integrity even if it has to be interrupted by the heavy wooden crossbars needed to support some doors (see Fig 1). Office doors frequently have clear glass, but stained glass can give a touch of class to that otherwise uninteresting entrance (see Fig 2). Or, a storm-door window can be made of stained glass. Stained-glass panels in doors must be especially sturdy, because the door will be frequently jarred. The panels can be strengthened by incorporating support rods into the panel that extend into the door frame, and also by pushing an adequate amount of putty between the glass and the lead leaf to ensure that the glass is held securely in position.

Fig 1   The wood panels in this door have been replaced with stained glass. The design used in a door should be strong enough to keep its effect even though split and divided by wood

## Shutters

Window shutters offer another setting for stained glass compositions. There are shutter frames on the market that are designed to be used with fabric inserts. Shutter frames can also be used to hold stained-glass inserts, and this makes a striking window treatment (see Fig 3). During daylight hours the brilliant colours cast a radiance over the interior, but if more light is desired, the panels can be opened. At night, light from within the home illuminates the glass, making it

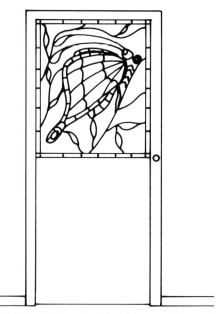

Fig 2  Stained glass in office doors provides privacy and can brighten up an area. This butterfly is used in the office door of an entomologist

Fig 3  A continuous design in these shutters makes the eye look past the framework and see not four small panels but one composition

glow like jewels, casting a spell over the neighbourhood.

*Screens*
Screens come in all shapes and sizes and can be used throughout the house. Screen partitions make an area feel open due to the flow of light through the glass, while still giving the impression of privacy. Glass screens usually don't reach from floor to ceiling. They might be suspended from the ceiling and not extend to the floor, or they might rest on the floor and reach only part way to the ceiling. An open feeling can best be obtained if the glass in the screen is light in colour and transparent (cathedral or antique glass), and also if holes or open areas are left in the screen design.

A small bathroom can be divided into functional areas with a stained-glass screen. For example, the toilet might be separated from the bath or sink to create areas of privacy. Likewise, a screen might be used in a kitchen to divide the work area from the dining space — perhaps a design of canned goods on shelves with the open areas located where the shelves are empty. Strategically positioned screens in a sitting room can also create the illusion of space. It is important to design screens with the desired effect in mind. Colour conveys a psychologically powerful message and must be used very carefully to complement an area's decor and mood rather than impose another conflicting element.

A screen can also be used in front of a fireplace (see Fig 4). It is not advisable to use it directly in front of the fire, but rather as a second screen through which the light might dance. During the summer when the fire-place is not in use, the screen can be lit from behind with an electric light.

*Suncatchers en masse*
Have you ever seen a large picture window virtually converted into a study of flowers or birds with simple suncatchers? Multiple suncatchers artistically placed

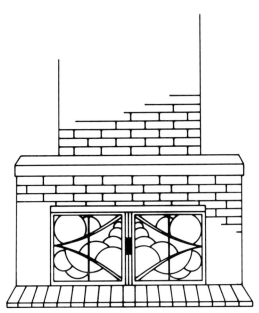

Fig 4   Use a stained-glass screen in front of a fire-place to pick up the dancing light from the fire

Fig 5   Stained glass can be used in cabinet doors

in a large window can be breathtaking. Suncatchers displayed en masse are usually more effective if a single subject is developed, but a variety of themes might be used to depict events in the lives or the hobbies of the owners.

You can build a collection of suncatchers for a dear friend or relative: each occasion (birthday, Christmas, etc) can be marked with a new suncatcher, — and you will not have to suffer the chore of looking for the 'right' gift.

*Kitchen, china and other cabinets*
Stained glass can be used in the doors of cabinets to hide unsightly items including irregular dishes and serving ware or to hide things of great value such as a collection of rare silver or glassware. When lit from within, the cabinet serves as a light box illuminating the art-glass doors. A cabinet panel might be elaborate or it may be a simple quarried or diamond pattern made with various colours of glass. Whatever the design, stained-glass doors will hide the contents of a cabinet while adding colour to a setting (see Fig 5). They can be highlighted with just a touch of coloured glass around the edges for yet another effect.

*Café doors*
Swinging 'café doors' are an interesting place for glass, providing a physical barrier which is visually stimulating (see Fig 6).

*Windows*
Some window locations are obviously just right for stained glass — these include stairwells, landings on staircases, and the ends of long narrow rooms, but many other sites work equally well. For instance, stained glass can be used to hide unsightly areas. If a window opens onto an alley or looks out on a neighbour's washline, hide it with something beautiful. This works nicely when homes are close together. Surprisingly, there is adequate light to illuminate a window even when buildings are only four to six

11

Fig 6    Art-glass panels in swinging 'café doors'

feet apart, as in many of the older sections of cities.

Stained glass can also be used to provide privacy. For years homes have had frosted or crinkled glass in bathroom windows, but a bathroom window is a perfect place to use stained glass. It gives the room privacy and at the same time adds to the decor. For a bit of privacy combined with a view of the outdoors, the stained glass might cover only the lower half of the window, leaving clear glass in the upper portion. This arrangement also allows the window to be opened. Or have a stained-glass design surrounded by clear glass, or conversely a central area of clear glass bordered by stained glass (see Figs 7 and 8).

It is important to study the intensity of light before designing a window and selecting glass for a particular location. Windows facing east or west will have a completely different quality of light from those facing north.

Stained-glass windows are usually large panels that fit into openings customarily filled with clear glass. However, some windows are divided into small sections, and it might be desirable to retain the sectioned look. To accomplish this, a design can be separated into many small units, and these are set in front of, or over, the existing window (see Figs 7 and 8). One advantage of this arrangement is that the narrow air space between the clear glass and the stained glass produces an insulating effect. A disadvantage is that the window cannot be readily moved to another location.

*Stained glass for basement windows*
In many homes basements have been converted into family or recreation rooms, and sometimes even a guest room is nestled at the foot of the stairs. It is always a challenge to convert those little rectangular windows that characterize basements (and detract from the decor) into positive features. Stained glass can be used to meet that challenge, but the windows must be designed with great sensitivity. They should reflect the mood or function of the room or mirror the personalities that people them. For instance, my desk is in the basement of my home, and I feel somewhat isolated when sequestered among my books and papers. I designed a couple of kids to share my solitary hours and they peer in the window and add a touch of warmth and cheer to my office. Windows can be designed to enhance and complement any decor. Visualize a sitting room with an abstract or traditional design, or a recreation room with perhaps an assortment of balls or other stylized recreational equipment, maybe a child's play area with a dog or cat scratching at the window, or a den with a ship or other subject that appeals to the resident.

Stained glass is a natural for basement windows. It provides privacy, can hide unsightly areas, and can convert a dreary window into a light-filtering art object. Because basement windows are located next to the ground, they are hard to keep clean and frequently have annoying mud spots, bits of grass or other debris stick-

12

Fig 7 & 8   The panels that make up these large windows contain stained-glass designs surrounded by clear glass (marked 1'). This decorating trick introduces art glass into a window yet retains a view of the outdoors and the flow of natural light

13

Small basement windows can be converted to bright pleasurable areas with stained glass

ing to them. If the windows are covered with stained glass, the dirt can't be seen (probably one reason many homeowners use 'stained-glass' contact paper on their basement windows), but fake glass is a poor substitute for the real thing.

Usually basement windows are in the outside walls of the house and transmit light only during daylight hours. Sometimes though, especially in older homes, extra rooms have been added, enlarging the foundations and leaving a darkened window on an interior wall. A low-wattage light can be placed behind the window under the extension in the unexcavated area so that the stained glass can be lit during the day as well as at night.

When installing a stained-glass panel, place it about 1in (25mm) from the inside of the basement window. This not only conserves energy, but it also protects the art glass — its nearness to the ground makes it vulnerable to a flying rock or a rolling ball.

By applying a little ingenuity at ground level, you can create unusual and interesting stained-glass windows for basements and enliven an otherwise dull area with line and colour.

## Other Uses of Glass

Here are just a few more ways glass might be used.

Wind chimes. Glass drills are available to make holes in the glass pieces so they can be hung from wire or string

Tissue boxes

Picture frames

Personal items, including jewellery such as necklaces, pins, pendants, and belt buckles

Trinket cases

Bird houses and feeders

Table tops

Candle holders

Planters and terraria

Lanterns

Lampshades, for hanging lamps, table lamps, floor lamps and night lights

Valances

Signs for advertising and club or company symbols

Weathervanes

Insertions in weaving and macramé

Borders for mirrors

Skylights

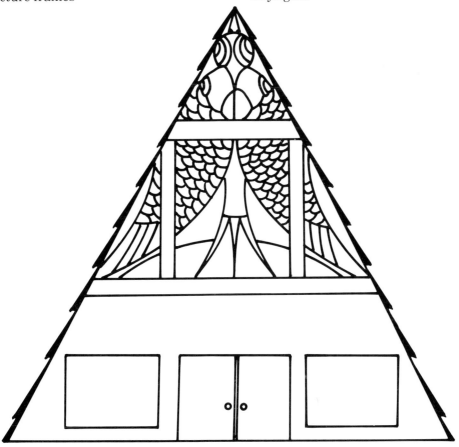

Fig 9  For a unique and dramatic dwelling, fill gables of an A-frame structure with a captivating design of stained glass

False ceilings

Suncatcher 'trees': suncatchers displayed on natural branches and suncatchers as Christmas-tree ornaments

Wall hangings

Glass walls or murals. These can also be used in the open space above kitchen cabinets or as a partition in an entry hall

Mobiles

## Holiday Cottages

Holiday cottages, summerhouses and small outdoor sitting areas can be made special with stained glass. Even used sparingly it can add immeasurably to the pleasure of the dwelling. One especially daring example using glass in a holiday home is shown in Fig 9. Clear glass is usually used in the gables of A-frame buildings, but it is very difficult to reach and keep clean. Dirty glass looks tacky unless, of course, it happens to be stained glass. One of the beauties of using stained glass is that dirt is barely perceptible, and as in the case of the magnificent windows in cathedrals, it actually intensifies the depth of colour. This feature should be considered when you decide how to handle hard-to-reach and hard-to-clean windows. Let stained glass solve the problem while simultaneously increasing the beauty of the cottage. (But don't be mislead. Stained glass does need care, otherwise acidic city fumes will cause surprisingly rapid decay.

## Free-hanging Art-glass Panels

Throughout the centuries stained glass has been used as a permanent installation to fill openings and it was considered an architectural art. But times have changed — glass has become mobile and attracted artists who are challenging the link between stained glass and architecture. Stained glass can be used to create free-hanging panels that are astonishingly powerful. It becomes more than a craft. Glass used to make artistically powerful statements is a fine art, one you might strive to develop once the basic techniques are conquered.

Many stained-glass artists consider windows to be extensions of walls, and they create art work to hang against the glass walls. Rejecting the architectural necessity of filling an opening, art panels can be made to hang in windows where the compositions are framed by the scenery of passing vehicles, grazing cows, the skyline, or birds in flight. These panels are not a permanent part of a building, and that is the key to their success. Ours is a mobile society with most people inhabiting a succession of homes and apartments. Many homeowners have had sadly to leave their prized stained-glass windows behind when they move. The new free-hanging stained-glass panels are not permanent installations and they are as easy to move and relocate as paintings. For this reason, many people are attracted to the new glass art and are acquiring it along with other works of art.

Although you are probably only now learning to work with glass, look ahead to what your future might hold. Stained glass sells. Suncatchers and other small items sell for pocket money, but there is more than small change to be made with stained glass. Glass art sells for significant sums. The advantages of making free-hanging art glass are numerous, the most obvious one being that you can function as an artist rather than as a decorator, and you are not required to coordinate your art work with someone's curtains or furniture. Also, free-hanging compositions often do not have exacting size requirements, like architectural glass. On the other hand, it's only wise to be flexible: it would not be expedient to forego a nice commission just because the customer wants a piece of glass art to fit a specific area!

Free-hanging stained-glass art is a new market and there are several tricks to successfully getting into it. First, of course, you need to create exciting art.

COLOUR PLATE
Three-dimensional Woodpecker on Wood (page 95)

16

And then with careful planning you can develop and nurture your clientele. One way to attract a following is to develop a style or theme that can always be recognized as your work. For instance, I have selected social comment as a theme and although my style changes as I grow as an artist, the thought-content of my compositions remains recognizable. This theme is satisfying because it gives me an opportunity to express thoughts about social issues. Although my panels are quite small, they sell (mid 1980s) for £125-£1200 ($200-$2000), with customers returning to add to their collections. But that doesn't just happen. You must make people want your work. To do this you must orchestrate your reputation as an artist. Make your debut with a formal showing, and if you can get a few pieces placed in the homes of art patrons and/or prominent citizens, your reputation will quickly spread. Never miss an opportunity to do an exhibit, and keep entering shows and gathering awards.

Be consistent with pricing. Ask more for better pieces, not because they are intricate or large, but because they are better than some of your other works. Stained-glass compositions have in the past usually been priced by the square foot, but an increasing number of glass artists are insisting that the price must be based on quality, as with other art objects.

It's a good life getting paid to do the things you like to do best. So if you have a flair for art and learn to handle glass, this just might be your ticket for 'living happily ever after'.

COLOUR PLATE
Free-hanging Butterfly (page 104)

# 2   Glass — the Medium

The essential ingredient in this craft is the stained glass. It is composed of sand, soda, potash and various metal oxides. These ingredients are heated to approximately 2500°F (1370°C) so that the components become molten and are mixed together. After the glass has been formed into sheets, it is slowly cooled in annealing ovens, (glass cooled too quickly will be brittle). There is a wide range of glass colours, transparencies and textures available, and the quality of glass varies considerably among manufacturers.

The two basic methods of producing sheet glass are rolling and blowing. Rolled glass, as the name implies, is rolled between two metal rollers, and the resulting sheets are approximately ⅛in (3mm) thick throughout. Blown glass, sometimes called antique glass, is produced by the methods that were used hundreds of years ago. A blob of molten glass is blown via a long tube and powerful lungs into a cylinder approximately 3ft (1m) long and 1ft (30cm) in diameter. To convert the cylinder into a sheet of glass, the ends are first cut off. The bottom is called a rondel and is used for special effects in glass crafting. Next, the soft glass is cut with metal shears along one side of the open-ended cylinder and is then placed on its side in a reheating oven where it opens out and becomes a flat sheet of glass.

Antique glass is usually softer than rolled glass, making it easier to score, but its thickness is sometimes irregular due to the method of production. It is usually thinner than machine-rolled glass, but sometimes it is quite thick, up to ¼in (6mm). It may have other variations, including bubbles, ripples and striations, all of which add interest to glass compositions. Antique glass is available in especially brilliant colours or as clear or transparent glass. Some antique glass is produced with streaks and swirls of different colours.

Another type is flashed glass, which has a thick base of clear or coloured glass with a very thin layer (the flashed layer) of another colour over it. Flashed glass is always cut on the thick side. It can be used to produce an unusual effect in stained-glass compositions. A protective covering such as contact paper is applied to the glass on the side with the flash coating. A pattern is cut from the protective covering and then the thin layer of flashed glass that is exposed is removed with hydrofluoric acid producing a design the colour of the base glass surrounded by glass the colour of the flash. It's a nice technique, but one to consider using only after you master the basics.

There are two main types of rolled glass — opalescent and cathedral. Opalescent glass is translucent and, because it is a mixture of two or more colours, frequently has a marbled appearance. It is a versatile glass that is used in windows as well as other stained-glass projects. In windows, the glass transmits a soft glow on sunny as well as dark days. Because it is translucent rather than transparent, it may be used where it is desirable to obstruct the view. Lamp shades are usually made with opalescent glass because they produce an even glow and the light fixture and bulb cannot be seen. It is also used for panels and objects through which light does not pass, such as frames around mirrors, boxes, or wall hangings, because the colour of the glass is apparent not only when light is transmitted through it, but also when light is reflected from it. It is usually quite soft and easy to score and break.

Rolled cathedral glass is transparent. Forms are easily seen through coloured cathedral glass (though distorted) but, unlike opalescent glass, it does not reflect light. Therefore, colours are not obvious unless light passes through it. Because of this characteristic, cathedral glass is used for items through which light will pass, such as windows and suncatchers. It is a little harder than opalescent glass and therefore a bit more difficult to score and break. Nonetheless, this beautiful glass adds immeasurably to stained-glass compositions, and it surely should be incorporated into them. Whole window panels can be made from cathedral glass, or it can be used as accent glass within an opalescent composition.

Texture is another feature of rolled glass. Antique glass is smooth on both sides, but rolled glass sometimes has a regular patterned texture on one side. The texture is produced when the molten glass is passed beneath a roller with a patterned surface; the other side of the glass remains smooth, to provide a surface for scoring. Many artists believe the regularity of the imprinted pattern detracts from the beauty of the glass, while others prefer textured glass in their compositions. A surface pattern produced by the roller method does not significantly affect the handling properties of glass.

There is also some special glass that has hand-produced textures. While the glass is molten it is cranked by hand through rollers to give it an uneven surface, or it is stirred and folded to produce an undulating and very irregular surface. All glass that is textured by hand comes in one-of-a-kind sheets. These are usually very beautiful and add considerable interest to an item, but most of them are expensive and very difficult to cut. It is wise to learn the skills of glass crafting with less demanding glass.

Glue chip, or frosted glass is another unusual glass. The surface has irregular frost patterns that are produced when the glass is covered with glue and then reheated. The glue alters the surface of the glass producing unusual swirls and configurations. It's an interesting glass but more difficult to score and break. Although more expensive, glue chip is worth the extra effort and cost when a special effect is wanted.

## The Basic Types and Characteristics of Glass

*Machine-rolled*
1 Regular thickness, about ⅛in (3mm)
2 Smooth on both sides or smooth on one side and textured on the other
3 Main types:
  a) Cathedral
  i) Transparent but murky
  ii) Clear or coloured, sometimes streaked with two or more colours, sometimes seedy (contains air bubbles)
  iii) Glue chip — frosted effect with irregular pattern
  b) Opalescent
  i) Translucent, often marbled
  ii) Two or more colours in swirls and streaks, rarely a single colour
  iii) The density or amount of light that can be transmitted through the glass will vary. The same colour may be available in several densities

*Antique or blown*
1 Transparent and brilliant with 'imperfections'
2 Smooth on both sides
3 Soft — easy to score and break
4 Colours: a) solid — clear or a single colour; b) streaky — two or more colours in swirls and streaks
5 Irregular thickness but usually thinner than rolled glass
6 Flashed glass — two layers, one very thin coating over a thicker base

*Hand-rolled*
1 Very irregular surface on one side, flat on the other
2 Usually small pieces or sheets
3 Difficult to score and break

4  Irregular thickness
5  Unique one-of-a-kind sheets

**Buying Glass**

Glass is priced by weight, so a square foot (or square metre) of thin glass will cost less than a similar sheet of thicker glass. Rolled opalescent and cathedral glass cost approximately the same. Blown antique glass is expensive to produce but, because it is considerably thinner than most rolled glass, it is not always a great deal more expensive per sheet.

The best source is a glass factory or supply house. Even if a shop that sells stained glass is in your vicinity, the cost will be much more than if you order directly from supply houses, even though they might require a minimum order. To acquire a supply of glass, order a glass sample kit. (Yes, you'll have to pay even for the samples.) This kit will contain small pieces of all the kinds of glass the company can supply. It is useful to make a panel to display them, with the number or name of each sample clearly visible. Place clear glass in an old picture frame and secure strips of wide zinc came across the frame from one side to the other. Place the samples in the groove of the came and let them rest against the clear glass. You might want to put another sheet of clear glass over the samples to secure them in position. Locate this display so the samples can be seen in natural light. When ordering glass or selecting it for a composition, refer to this panel to judge colours and glass interactions.

Professionals buy glass in stock or half-stock sheets, which vary in size depending on the manufacturer (square-foot sheets are common). When buying, don't order a piece of this and a piece of that, because you will end up with lots of pretty glass but without enough of any one colour to lend continuity to a composition, or to serve as a background glass. Order multiple sheets of a few basic subdued shades along with single sheets of a variety of colours. The cost of the different colours reflects the cost of the chemical compounds that are used to produce the colour in the glass. Blues, greens, and browns cost less than reds and yellows. Before ordering glass, have in mind how it will be used in a project.

One or two words of caution. A sheet of glass may have many variations in colour. For this reason, a small sample may be misleading. Experience is the best way to learn about the colours and the qualities of glass; so order some, and then base future orders on the experience you gain. Also, glass from different factories varies considerably. Glass from one factory may be much better to work with than glass from another factory. Usually the glass from a given factory will have specific characteristics: it may be hard, soft, or brittle; it may score easily and break consistently, or it may be erratic in its working qualities. Again, experience is your best teacher and it's wise to experiment with a variety of glass.

British stockists sell 8 x 12in (20 x 30cm) pieces of glass for the hobby market, and you can buy glass cut to your required size at a 20 per cent surcharge.

Scrap glass can be purchased at stained-glass studios and craft shops for a fraction of the full-sheet cost. Sometimes the scraps are rather large and well worth picking up — they are known as cullet and can be bought by the pound. If you plan to make only small articles, it might be to your advantage to buy scrap glass. Even if you anticipate making large compositions, it is worth looking for scrap, because it is an opportunity to expand your glass stock with different colours and textures and to experience the different qualities of glass. A glass inventory is to a glass craftsman what a palette is to a painter; the larger it is, the better. Never dig through a box of scrap glass without protective gloves.

**Handling Glass**

Stained glass must be cautiously handled, as it is easily damaged, and it can be dangerous.

Use an old picture frame or ½in zinc came to make the frame for this display board. Place zinc came across the frame and fill the groove with glass samples, positioning them so that identifying numbers are visible. Hang the samples in natural light, perhaps in front of a window, as shown

This glass storage bin is made of plywood with partitions for segregating the glass. The partitions are of various heights and widths to accommodate different size sheets. Small pieces of glass are stored in clearly marked boxes with a single colour in each box

Small sheets of glass are easier to carry and store and are less dangerous than big ones. Usually sheets can be carried without incident, but occasionally one will, upon the slightest provocation, shatter or split apart. When purchasing glass, wear gloves for sorting through the sheets and picking scrap glass from bins. It is amazing how quickly a piece of glass can cause an injury and it's always wise to wear gloves for protection.

Never carry glass home unwrapped. Most suppliers wrap it without being asked, but if they don't, then ask them to do so. Carry glass sheets upright and carry scrap glass in a sturdy box.

## Storing Glass

When storing glass, stand the sheets on edge and lean them against a solid wall or surface at a slight angle. Place sheets of glass in a storage bin with the jagged edges to the back, and keep the area in front of the bin open and free of objects that might cause you to trip or fall against the glass. Never store glass overhead. It should also not be stored on damp or concrete floors which can affect its durability.

Glass should not be stacked, as sheets tend to slide against each other, or one piece might break and cause a domino reaction, with all the sheets within the pile breaking under the stress caused by the initial break. It may be inconvenient to put away each sheet of glass after use, but it is a wise practice which keeps the work area tidy and safe.

The storage bin should be divided into sections with wood partitions. Since the sheets are sold in various sizes, the storage sections should vary in both height and width. Use partitions to separate the different colours and types. Label the various slots with the colour name because, although the colour of opalescent glass can be determined while the glass is in the bin, most sheets of cathedral and antique all appear the same until they are pulled from the slots and held in front of a light. This is a time-consuming task that can be averted if the glass is stored in colour-labelled sections. Even so, it is necessary to study the glass, and this is best accomplished if a light is located so that the colour of the glass can be seen when just an edge is pulled from the storage bin. Store scrap glass in clearly labelled cigar or shoe boxes with a single colour in each box.

# 3 Tools and Supplies

There is some basic equipment needed to work with glass. Although you can get by with regular household tools such as pliers, nails, scissors, etc, it is wise to acquire the proper equipment because it will enable you to produce good-quality work, and encourage you to go on to bigger and better items. Poor or inadequate tools can cause frustration and, more likely than not, lead you to give up your stained-glass venture. But the proper tools will enforce good procedural practices that will result in successfully completed projects. Make an effort to obtain the following items.

## Pattern Shears

These unusual scissors are used to cut apart the pieces of pattern paper. The shears have two blades on the bottom and a single blade on top. They remove a strip of paper from between the pattern pieces as they are cut apart. There are two types of pattern shears, and the type that is used will depend upon whether the project is to be 'foiled' or 'leaded'. These two methods of construction will be discussed later. If the project is to be foiled, you use shears that remove a sliver of paper only $1/32$in (0.8mm) wide as they cut apart the pattern pieces. If the project is to be leaded, use shears that remove a sliver of paper $1/16$in (1.8mm) wide from between the pattern pieces. The width of the sliver of paper is the amount of space that the foil or lead will occupy between the pieces of glass. Regular household scissors can be used if pattern shears are not available (see Chapter 4).

## Glass-breaking Pliers

These invaluable pliers have wide flat jaws for gripping the glass. They are used to hold glass when breaking or pulling apart large pieces along a scored line. If glass-breaking pliers are not available, regular pliers can be used to hold small pieces of glass during the breaking process and larger pieces can be gripped between the fingers and thumb of each hand (see Techniques).

## Grozing Pliers

These are used to nibble away small fragments of glass, and are essential for breaking out the glass of a concave or inner curve of scored glass. They are also used instead of glass-breaking pliers to hold a very small piece of glass while breaking it along a scored line. Grozing away irregularities from larger pieces of glass can also be accomplished by using the notched side of a glass cutter (see Chapter 4).

## Soldering Iron

Beginners have a tendency to buy a low-wattage inexpensive iron only to find that more heat is needed as their work becomes more sophisticated and requires extended periods of soldering. If you are serious about your commitment to stained-glass craft, buy a 100-150 watt iron with an iron-clad tip. Soldering-iron tips that transfer heat most efficiently and produce the smoothest joints are made of copper, but iron-clad tips are longer-lasting, and for this reason are used by many hobbyists and most professionals. The disadvantage of copper tips is that they need 'dressing' more frequently than plated tips. This means that the soldering edge loses its shape after extended use and it must be reshaped by filing or grinding against a grinding wheel. Even so, many master craftspeople prefer copper tips; they do yield excellent results.

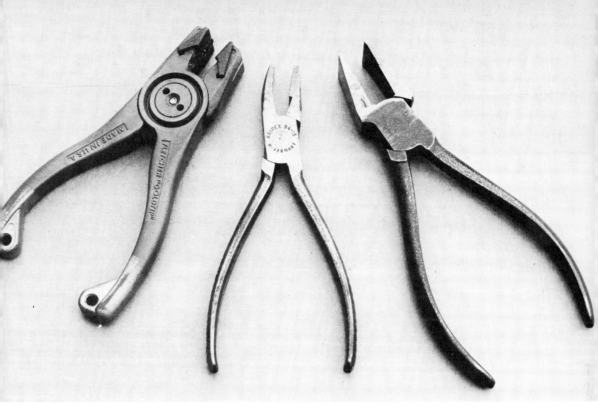

(*from the left*) Running pliers for long straight breaks, grozing pliers to nibble off tiny pieces of glass, and wide-jaw breaking pliers for holding medium-size pieces of glass while breaking

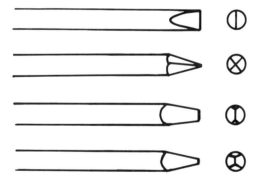

Fig 10   The four most popular shapes of soldering-iron tips are (from the top): chisel, pyramid, and two widths of semi-chisel

The shape of soldering-iron tips varies, the three most common shapes being chisel, semi-chisel, and pyramid (see Fig 10). Select a shape based upon how it will be used. The pyramid is most versatile, because it has a point as well as flattened sides; consequently it can be used for very fine or hard-to-reach areas, and also for seams and joints. The semi-chisel (wide) is the choice of most professionals, because the flat sides yield a large heated surface allowing an even flow of solder. The wide semi-chisel tip is also effective for making tidy joints between pieces of lead came.

The temperature of the soldering iron should be controlled by a rheostat. This will allow you to regulate the heat of the tip more sensitively. The rheostat controls the current that reaches the iron and will automatically limit the energy supplied to it, allowing you to leave the iron plugged in for extended periods of soldering without the risk of overheating. If the temperature of the soldering iron is uncontrolled, it may overheat and

27

A 100-150 watt soldering iron, solid-core solder, oleic acid flux and a stiff brush

melt the lead came; or the solder could become too fluid and fail to adhere to the surface being soldered. A rheostat can be placed in the electric cord of the soldering iron, or else the soldering iron can be plugged into a special rheostat unit. The former is quite efficient and costs much less.

## Solder
Several types of solder are used in stained-glass work, but the most versatile solder that can be used for a variety of projects is 60/40 solder; a mixture of 60 parts tin and 40 parts lead. In Britain this is sold by Fry's Metals under the name Blowpipe 'C'. This combination of metals becomes fluid at a relatively low temperature yet makes a strong bond when it cools. The solder should be $\frac{1}{8}$ in in diameter and have a solid core, meaning that it has no flux inside. Another popular solder is 50/50.

## Flux

Flux is a chemical that is applied to lead came or copper foil just before soldering. It prevents the formation of metal oxides as the metals are heated to a high temperature, thereby ensuring good adhesion between the solder and the metals being joined. Buy a small bottle of oleic-acid flux, and a small stiff brush with which to apply it. A more convenient method uses a tallow candle, available from most ironmongers. Simply rub this onto the clean joint before applying solder.

## Copper Foil

The 'copper-foil' technique of stained-glass construction is based upon the fact that copper is pliable and solder readily adheres to it. A thin strip of copper is secured around the edge of each piece of glass. The pieces of glass are then placed in position and the copper foil along the edge of one piece of glass is soldered to the copper foil on the adjoining piece of glass, creating a seam that joins the glass together as a unit. Foil is available as thin ribbons of copper, packaged on spools. The most popular widths range from 5/32in to 1/2in. Generally, the narrower foil is used for small intricate projects and wider foil for larger projects, because it affords added strength. The copper-foil ribbon has an adhesive on one side which, when placed against the edge of the glass, causes the foil to stick to the glass.

## Lathekin (Larupin)

A lathekin or larupin is a small tapered piece of wood or plastic used to smooth the copper against the edge and surface of the glass. It is very useful for widening the came channel before inserting the glass.

## Lead Came

Lead came is sometimes used instead of copper foil between pieces of glass. Generally, it is used for large projects such as windows, because it gives better support than copper foil within the composition. Lead is flexible and can be bent to con-

form to the edges of the glass pieces. Came is placed between each piece of glass and holds the glass in position with an overlapping lip. The lead pieces are held together with solder at each point of intersection. The strips of lead came come in two basic shapes in cross-section, 'H' and 'U'. H-shaped came has a groove or channel on each side, into which the glass fits. It is used as a common border wherever two pieces of glass are butted together, as within a window panel. U-channel lead came has only one channel, and is used around the outer edge of items such as suncatchers or small windows.

Came is available in many widths and shapes. The width of the came refers to the size of the overlay or leaf and not to the heart or inner core which remains of constant thickness. Poor fit caused by inaccurately cut glass can be concealed under the overlapping leaf of wide lead, and for this reason, beginners should not attempt to use a narrow width. As you become more proficient with the materials and learn to cut glass accurately, a narrower leaf can be used. Wide lead makes small items too bulky, so use 1/8 or 3/16in came for suncatchers and other small articles. On the other hand, wide came provides added support and should be used on larger windows. Glass pieces in panels not larger than 2 x 3ft (0.6-1.0m)

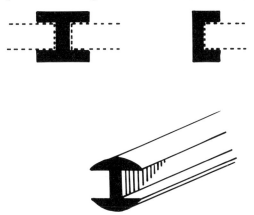

Fig 11   H-channel and U-channel lead came. The overleaf may be flat or curved as shown

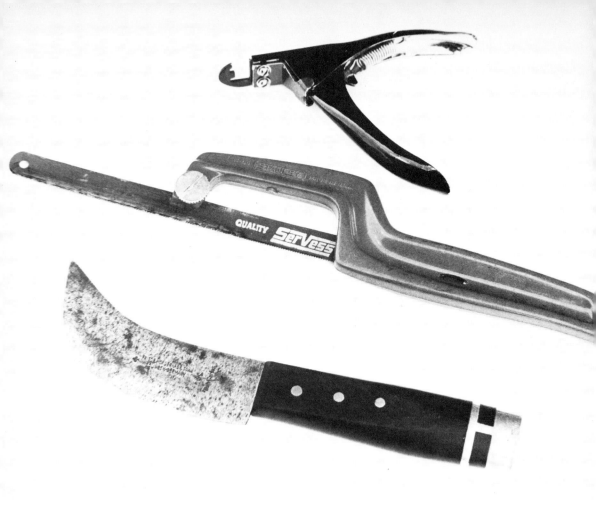

Lead can be cut with a variety of implements including (from below) a lead knife, hacksaw blade and lead snips

are frequently joined together with ¼in wide H-channel, but a wider came should be used for larger panels. Came also varies in the shape of the overleaf. It may be flat or curved on the top and bottom surfaces (see Fig 11).

### Zinc Came

Zinc came is also available in the U- or H-channel shape and different widths. Zinc adds strength to a composition and for this reason, it is wise to place zinc came around the perimeter of panels. If a panel is quite large and there might be a tendency for internal weakness or sagging, zinc came should be placed at strategic locations within the panel as well as around it. Zinc is not flexible like lead and for this reason it can be used only on straight or nearly straight lines.

Of course, this poses no problem when using it to surround a straight-edged window panel. Use a wide zinc around large panels, and narrow zinc around small ones.

## Lead Knife
A lead knife is shaped somewhat like a linoleum cutter, except the sharp edge is the outer convex margin rather than the inner concave edge. The blade is held against the lead and rocked back and forth with light pressure applied until the lead came is severed. A sawn-off putty knife makes a cheaper lead knife which can be shaped to your preference.

A hacksaw blade can also be used for cutting lead and in fact does not distort the lead as much as the knife does. But it takes longer to use and for this reason is not the preferred tool.

Lead snips are a useful device, the quickest and neatest way to achieve a right-angle cut through lead came. But they are not adequate for making acutely angled cuts. Therefore, both the knife and the snips are recommended for cutting lead.

## Horseshoe Nails
These nails, also called glazing nails, have flattened sides which effectively hold pieces of glass in position as work progresses. Horseshoe nails aren't essential for glass work, but they will make it proceed much more smoothly than if regular nails are used. It is advisable to put a snippet of lead came between glass and nail to avoid shelling and chipping.

## Scoring Board
You need to lay the glass on a sturdy piece of plywood ½-¾in (12-20mm) thick while you score it. A handy board size is 18 x 24in (45 x 60cm), but it must be large enough to accommodate the largest sheets of glass used. Larger pieces of glass are used by professionals — up to 3 x 6ft (1 x 2m) sheets — but these are unwieldy and not advisable for the non-professional, being quite dangerous to

handle. Most craftspeople work with glass sheets that will easily fit on an 18 x 24in (45 x 60cm) board. Nail a thin strip of wood along one edge of the board as a stop, so you can push the glass against it while scoring.

## Building Board
Leaded stained-glass panels should be constructed on a building board, its size being determined by the size of the panel to be made. It is convenient to have several boards ranging in size from 2 x 3ft (0.6 x 1.0m) to 4 x 8ft (1.2 x 2.4m). Cut a building board from ¾-1in (20-25mm)

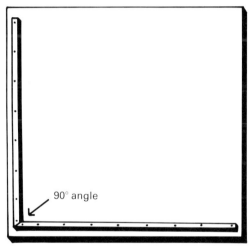

90° angle

Fig 12   Building board

plywood. Nail a strip of wood about ¾ x ½in (20 x 12mm) along two adjacent edges making a 90 degree angle on the corner of the board — on the left for a right-handed person, or on the right if you are left-handed. The precision of the angle is critical because it is against these strips that the two adjacent sides of a panel or window will be constructed. If the angle at the corner of the building board is not square, the projects constructed on the board will not have square corners (see Fig 12).

## Glass Cutter
There are many types of glass cutters on

31

the market as well as glass-cutting saws. A glass saw is basically a band saw, but these are prohibitively expensive for the hobbyist. Glass cutters are quite adequate for stained-glass work. They all work on essentially the same principle. A small-diameter wheel turns on an axle at the end of a handle. When the wheel is pressed and pulled against the glass, it revolves and scores the glass. This simple device is a remarkable improvement over the medieval equipment used for breaking glass. Early stained-glass craftsmen broke glass by drawing a hot iron along the line where a break was to be made: the heat caused the glass to crack. It was not possible to make intricate cuts with this crude method and that is why early stained-glass windows were, for the most part, made up of large pieces of coloured glass, with much of the design painted onto the surface.

Many modern stained-glass hobbyists prefer a simple and inexpensive pattern cutter, such as a Shaw or Fletcher Number 8. The steel wheels on these are 5/32in in diameter, and specially designed to cut around sharp curves. Some cutters have a steel ball on the end of the handle that is used to tap along the scored line,

Fig 13 Use the notched edge of the glass cutter to nibble away bits of glass

but on the opposite side of the glass. This light tapping encourages the glass to break along the scored line.

One edge of the cutter is notched, the notches being about 1/8in (3mm) wide. Each notch fits over the edge of the glass and can be used to nibble away bits of glass (see Fig 13), but grozing pliers are much more effective. Keep the cutter lubricated by standing it in a small jar containing about 1/2in (12mm) of a mixture of 1 part household oil and 2 parts kerosene. Put several layers of cloth in the bottom of this jar to protect the cutting wheel and discard the cutter when it becomes dull or nicked.

## Grinding Wheel

Works of finer quality and greater detail can be produced if the glass pieces are finished on a grinding wheel to remove snags and to make the edges square with the surface of the glass. This process is particularly important when making small foiled items because jagged edges on the glass can prevent one piece of glass fitting snugly to another. Grinding the edge of the glass is usually not necessary if the project is leaded, because the lead leaf or overlay covers the irregularities.

The grinding wheels available in craft shops are designed especially for glass work. Water splashing against the wheel keeps the abrasive wheel clean and the glass cool, preventing the glass from chipping while it is being ground. A heavy-duty grinder with a 1/8 HP motor and a diamond cutting-head is the usual choice for the home worker. The diamond head will last for around 200 hours of grinding. Each head has several grinding positions and each position lasts for about 50 hours of grinding. This means that thousands of pieces of glass can be ground with a diamond head before it needs replacement. A diamond grinder does not injure the skin if it is inadvertently touched.

A regular workshop belt-driven grinder can also be used without undo hardship, but glass tends to chip when ground against a wheel unlubricated with water and requires much more sensitive handling. Nonetheless, it can be done and is advised if a water-lubricated grinder designed for glass work is not available. The composition of the workshop grinding wheel is important. Use a wheel made of aluminium oxide with vitrified grit number 60 (medium), or a carborundum wheel. The wheel can be 3-6in (7.5-15cm) in diameter — the latter being the more desirable size. A workshop grinding wheel with an electric motor is a versatile tool that can be used for purposes other than stained-glass work.

If you can't manage to acquire either kind of grinding wheel, then use a hand-held grinding stone to smooth the irregular edges of the glass. It's tedious work but it can be done; in fact this technique was used for several of the projects shown in this book.

### Light Table

A light table will enable you to see and ponder the colours of the glass to be used in a project before the work is soldered together. Working without a light table is like working in the dark, since you can't see how a panel or window is progressing until after it is soldered together and finally held up to the light. This can be a moment of joy or it can be a rude awakening! Too often, when working without a light table, a few pieces of glass that lack the right colour or character find their way into a composition. At this point, with the pieces already soldered together, it is a big chore to unsolder them and remove the offending glass. More often than not, you simply leave the wrong glass in place and the whole project suffers.

A light table is only a box on legs with lights in the bottom of the box and a clear or frosted surface on the top. Incandescent light imparts a yellow hue to stained glass, but the light from fluorescent tubes approaches natural light as it is transmitted through glass. Perhaps the easiest way to make a light table is to make a table frame and put a shelf about 18in (45cm) below the top. Lay fluorescent fixtures upside down on the shelf. Make the surface of the table of plexiglass or ¼in (6mm) frosted glass. Cover the plexiglass with frosted contact paper or tracing paper to diffuse the light. Copper-foiled panels will be soldered together on the light-table surface, so if the top is made of plexiglass, lay a sheet of clear glass over it to prevent heat damage while soldering.

Plexiglass or
frosted glass

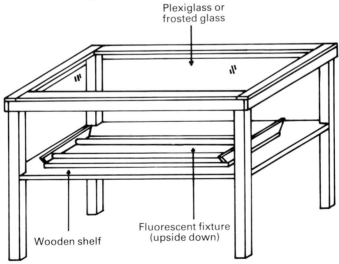

Wooden shelf

Fluorescent fixture
(upside down)

Fig 14   Light table

33

Leaded panels are constructed on a board, because nails are needed to hold the pieces in position during construction, and the nails cannot be driven into the top of the light table. Glass that is being considered for use in leaded panels should be laid out on a light table first, for study; you can then see how the various pieces interact. Some workers cut all of the glass in a leaded composition and look at it in position on the light table before moving it to a building board to be leaded and soldered together.

The size of the light table will affect the size of the projects you undertake. A table 3 x 4ft (1 x 1.3m) is versatile, but small tables or boxes are adequate for less adventurous endeavours. Make the table as large as will conveniently fit into your work area. To avoid having another large table around, the building board for leaded projects can be used on top of the light table.

**Unusual Inclusions**
Personalize your compositions by incorporating unusual items. Many textures and substances are compatible with stained glass and can be used in conjunction with it to make an interesting work. The following examples illustrate how several items have been used, and are presented here to encourage you to be innovative.

The clown pictured in this book (page 157) is a life-size panel and the clown displays a glass eye that was worn by a long-deceased member of my family. After the panel was completed, I realized that a large pearl button instead of a glass nugget would have been perfect at the end of the clown's suspenders. Another panel, Janet (page 161), has tiny bone-china roses holding the lock of hair. This type of fine detail is more noticeable in wall hangings where the surface of the glass is observed than in windows where light shines through. Even so, interesting objects can be used effectively in windows. You might include buttons, eye glasses, an old watch, shells, beautiful marbles, jewellery, buckles and maybe keys. Lenses from cameras and magnifying glasses can also give an unusual touch: concave and convex lenses alter the image of objects beyond the glass, sometimes inverting the image and producing an extraordinary effect (see Energy panel, page 164). But a word of caution about lenses. They must not be used in windows exposed to intense rays of the sun, because they might concentrate the light rays and cause a fire. Lenses should preferably be used in windows facing north.

What else might be included? Perhaps reflectors and tail lights from cars, mirrors, thin slices of transluscent stone — whatever appeals to your imagination. There are no rules, so be original.

**Suppliers**
Equipment, supplies, and glass can be purchased from supply houses and craft shops, but it would be wise to compare prices because of the great variation in the market. To purchase everything recommended would require a considerable investment, but most of the items will enhance your work for many years. It is much easier to work when you have the proper tools, but if tools must be acquired slowly, work can proceed with makeshift implements. Several items in this book were made from scrap glass using only a glass cutter, regular pliers, a low-wattage soldering iron, and a hand-held grinding stone (see Suppliers, page 169).

COLOUR PLATE
Parrot in Ring (page 113)

# 4   Stained-glass Techniques

The procedure for creating in stained glass consists of (1) making a design; (2) enlarging the design to the desired size, thereby making a cartoon; (3) making a pattern by copying the cartoon; and (4) cutting the pattern pieces apart to serve as glass-cutting patterns. Next, (5) the glass is cut to fit each pattern piece. Then (6), the glass pieces are assembled, either by placing copper foil along the edges of each piece of glass or by fitting lead came between the pieces of glass. Soldering the seams of the copper-foiled glass or the intersections of the lead came surrounding the glass holds the composition together as a unit. If lead came is used, it is necessary (7) to push putty under the came leaf where it overlaps onto the glass. If copper foil is used to hold the pieces of glass together, (8) a chemical finish may be applied to the soldered lines to produce an old or antique appearance. Finally, (9) the item must be thoroughly cleaned. In the following sections, each of these procedures is explained and illustrated.

## Making the Design

A large number and variety of designs are included in this book. Before making original designs, it will be instructive for you to study those later in this book to discover how lines intersect, and the role lines play not only as a means of dividing the glass into cuttable units, but also as integral parts of the design. Rectangles, diamonds and other patterns are sometimes used in the background to divide it into pieces that can be cut from glass (see Fig 15).

Several points should be kept in mind

when designing for stained glass. Strive for simplicity. A line that can be drawn with a swish of a pencil represents the edges of two pieces of glass, one on either side of the line. Each piece of glass must be cut to conform to the line, and then joined together either with foil or lead that is then soldered together. Clearly, each line in a cartoon represents a lot of work to be done when constructing the composition. Simplicity makes constructing the article easier. But there is a more important reason why simplicity helps. Nice flowing lines make a clean-looking composition, but a small intricate pattern without areas of contrast makes an item look cluttered. The beauty and qualities of glass cannot be captured through the union of many little pieces of glass, so try to use small pieces mixed with larger ones.

To get ideas flowing, start doodling. If you are designing a window, draw on small pieces of paper of the same relative width and length as the window you are planning. For instance, if the window is to be 3 x 4ft, make the doodling area 3 x 4in, or if you prefer a larger pad, prepare sketch sheets 9 x 12in. Make numerous pieces of paper to the correct proportion so you will feel free to draw and discard until a pleasing pattern begins to emerge. Then work to refine it. Keep drawing and redrawing lines until you are satisfied. While making a drawing, consider where the window will be used and the feeling the window should convey. For instance, avoid putting a setting sun in a north window, for it would be very unsettling to people who possess a strong sense of direction. Stained-glass compositions will set the mood of an area and must be carefully designed to produce the desired effects.

COLOUR PLATE
Unicorn (page 117)

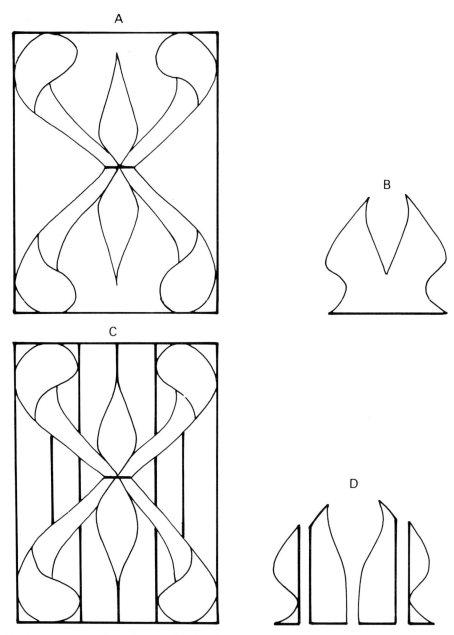

Fig 15  Design your panels so it is possible to cut the pieces of glass that make up the design. The background in design A would be virtually impossible to cut out (see B for the shape of one of the background pieces), but if the background is divided into units (as in C) the background is easily cut. Drawing D shows how the single piece of background glass in B can be divided into six easily cut pieces

After completing the design, let it rest for a few days before drawing it to scale. Place it where you will see it often through the day. Time will help reveal errors that, once in glass, will never cease to annoy you. When satisfied with the small design, you are ready to make a cartoon by drawing it to scale.

## Drawing the Cartoon

A cartoon is a line drawing of the proposed composition drawn to scale. Stained-glass articles are constructed over or on top of a cartoon. If the article will be assembled by the copper-foil method, the cartoon paper should be translucent, so that light from the light table can illuminate the cartoon and the glass placed over it as the work proceeds. Translucent paper or tracing paper can be bought in most art shops or stationers, by the piece or in pads of varying sizes.

If the stained-glass article is to be assembled by the lead-came method, use a sturdy paper stock for the cartoon, because the article will be constructed on a board rather than on a light table, and light is not passed through it during construction.

Some of the cartoons in this book are full-size and do not need to be enlarged, whereas other designs must be enlarged to make a cartoon. Whether you use a design from this book or one that you have developed yourself, it must be enlarged to scale, and this is readily accomplished by the grid method.

## Enlarging a Design

Small designs can be enlarged to any desired size to form a cartoon. First define the outer limits of the proposed cartoon with lines on the cartoon paper. Be sure the corners of the boundary lines are square — use a steel square or some other reliable drawing technique. The outer limits of the cartoon for a window or panel that is to fit into a specific opening should be slightly smaller on each edge than the opening itself — perhaps ⅛-¼in (3-6mm). Measure the window opening very carefully at the top and bottom and be certain that the opening is square. And remember that the outer border of the panel will consist of lead or zinc came that is generally considerably wider and stronger than the lead used within the panel. The edgemost pieces of stained glass will not reach the edge of the cartoon but will be inserted into the channel of the lead or zinc came which forms the panel edge.

The grid method is commonly used for enlarging a drawing to the desired cartoon size. A grid is a series of equally spaced horizontal and vertical lines. Draw a grid over the design to be enlarged. Draw another grid with the same number of units on the cartoon paper. If the design is to be enlarged, for instance, six times (eg to convert a 6 x 6in drawing to a 36 x 36in cartoon), then each section of the cartoon grid should be six times larger than the sections drawn over the small design. Number the horizontal and vertical lines so corresponding lines and sections in the large and the small grids can be easily located. Now you are ready to transfer the design, section by section, to the large grid, making adjustments as necessary (see Fig 16). It requires very little practice to enlarge accurately.

## Making a Pattern

It is necessary to make a copy of the cartoon to serve as the pattern for cutting the pieces of glass. The pattern should be made on poster paper, which is glossy on one side. Use a thickness the same as 3 x 5in postcards. Place the poster paper on a flat surface and lay carbon paper face-down over it. Next, place the cartoon over the carbon paper. Tack or tape all of the papers in position so they cannot shift while the cartoon is being copied. Using a sharp pencil, coloured — so you can tell the lines you have traced — carefully and firmly go over each line of the cartoon. Before separating the sheets of paper, number each of the pattern pieces. The numbering is of paramount importance, because the pieces are going to be cut

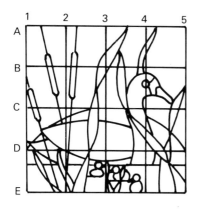

Fig 16  The grid method of enlarging a design

40

apart; the numbers will identify the location of each pattern piece, and the correct side. They may be numbered in any order.

If you use a full-size cartoon from this book and don't want to remove the page, then make two copies — one to serve as a cartoon over which the article will be constructed, and the other to be cut apart and used as the pattern. To do this, slip carbon paper behind the cartoon in this book, then add a piece of paper for the cartoon, then another piece of carbon, and lastly the light poster paper for the pattern. Trace over the cartoon in the book with a sharp coloured pencil and number each piece.

## Cutting Apart Pattern Pieces

The pattern pieces may be cut apart before glass cutting commences, or they can be cut apart as they are needed. If the composition has many pieces it is easier to keep track of the pieces if they aren't separated until needed, but this interrupts the glass cutting. If the pieces are all cut apart at once, be sure to keep them 'filed', or you will waste a lot of time trying to find them when you want them. Separate them into envelopes for pieces 1-10, 11-20 and so forth.

The method you use for cutting apart the pattern pieces will depend on the method you plan to use for joining together the pieces of glass. If the article is to be copper foiled, then cut the pieces apart and carefully *cut away the pencil line* between the pieces. This fine line is the amount of space needed to accommodate the foil that will be placed around the edge of the glass. If this fine line is not removed, then the foiled pieces of glass will be slightly too large and will not fit the cartoon exactly. This sliver of pattern paper can be removed by using the type of pattern shears mentioned among the tools in Chapter 3, or by cutting away the pattern line with regular household scissors as mentioned above.

If the article is to be held together with lead came, then cut the pieces apart with pattern-cutting shears designed for lead-

came projects. Shears designed for leaded projects remove a wider strip of paper from between the pattern pieces than those designed for foiled projects. This compensates for the width of the heart of the lead came that will be placed between the glass pieces.

However, if pattern shears for leaded projects are not available, regular scissors can be used if the following procedure is followed. Before cutting the pattern pieces apart with scissors, go over all the lines of the pattern with an unsharpened pencil; this will give a pencil line that is wide enough to compensate for the heart of the lead came. Remove the sliver of paper from between the pattern pieces by cutting on either side of the pencil line; or, in other words, cut away the pencil line. Thus, whichever technique is used for holding the glass pieces together, foiling or leading, a sliver of pattern paper must be removed from between the pattern pieces, but the width of that sliver of paper is determined by the glazing technique to be used — lead or foil.

## Selecting Glass

Creating with stained glass requires a different approach from creating with paints on a canvas. Designing the lines and the shape of the glass pieces is an essential part of the creativity needed for working with glass. An equally demanding task lies in selecting the glass to be used. Stained-glass artists must visualize interactions of colour and line before it is realized; they must select textures, colours, and qualities of glass and, in a sense, make a greater commitment to its use than a painter makes when selecting a colour. An oil or acrylic painter can easily change the colour within a composition by painting over an ill-conceived area, but a stained-glass artist wastes valuable glass and time when glass must be changed. Don't select all of the glass to be used in a piece before starting to work; instead, spend time contemplating the work before it begins and decide upon a general feel it should project. Select the glass as the work proceeds, basing each selection on the combinations and interactions of the glass as it is used, much as a painter selects colours based upon the developing needs of a painting. In order to do this effectively you must be totally familiar with the colours and textures of the glass that is stored in your glass bin. The glass bin is your palette and it requires constant attention — mixing and comparing glass in order to use it most effectively. So it is obvious that even if you use a ready-made design from this book, the finished product will contain elements of your creative capacity, because you will determine which glass to use and therefore establish the integrity of the piece.

## Scoring and Breaking Glass

After determining which glass to use, the next step is to cut each pattern piece from glass. The glass is first scored and then pulled apart. To score glass means to scratch a line upon its surface. The

Position the glass cutter with the handle against the web between the first and second fingers. Place your thumb on the opposite side of the handle and grip firmly, with fingers and thumb pressing against the finger rests. Allow the third and fourth fingers to rest against the glass, thereby stabilizing your hand. Score glass by pulling the cutter firmly towards your body

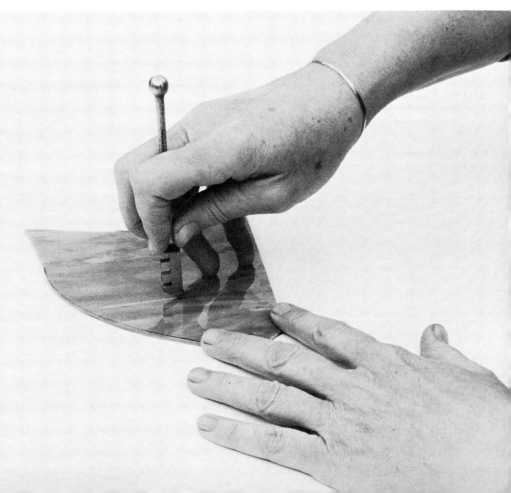

scratch or indentation becomes a line of weakness, and when pressure is applied on each side of it, the glass will break along it. You score glass with a glass cutter which (as described earlier) consists of a small bevel-edged wheel that turns on an axle at the end of a shaft or handle. There is no right way to hold a cutter; what works for one person doesn't work for the next. Nonetheless, the traditional manner of holding a cutter is with the shaft resting against the skin web between the first and second fingers and the thumb positioned on the opposing side of the shaft (see photograph). The fingers are held firmly against the flattened finger rest while the thumb pad presses against the thumb rest. Other techniques for holding the cutter may be equally effective for you, but however the cutter is held, the fingers must remain rigid.

Perhaps more important than the method of holding the cutter is the amount of energy used to roll the cutter across the glass. A great deal of strength is required to score the glass, and that strength must come from the shoulders

43

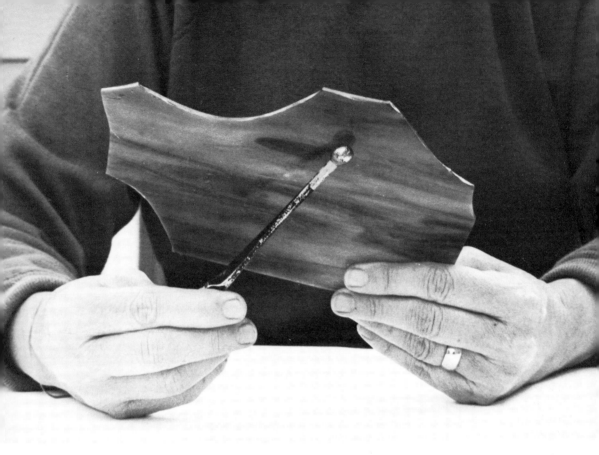

With the ball end of the cutter, tap along the scored line on the opposite side of the glass. The sound produced by tapping on the glass changes as the scored line runs through the glass

and arms, with the body moving to adjust for the shoulder movement. It is easiest to score glass while standing before a high table because the body can exert more force and move with the score lines. Do not use your fingers to guide the cutter along the pattern line because this will cause you to tire quickly. Some people pull the cutter towards them as they score glass, but others move the cutter away. When the cutter is pulled towards the body the hand sometimes covers the pattern and it is difficult to follow the lines without leaning over in a somewhat awkward position. Even so, this technique seems more satisfactory than moving the cutter away from the body, because the upper arm muscles have more strength in the pulling rather than the pushing movement. Still, it's a matter of trying the different methods and adopting the one that works best for you.

A skin-tingling crackle can be heard as

the cutter moves across the glass. It is important to break the glass soon after it has been scored because structural changes take place inside the glass after it is scored. If scored glass is left for long, the probability of a clean break decreases. After the glass has been scored, tap it along the score line on the opposite side of the glass with the ball end of the cutter. The sound produced by the tapping changes as the internal structure of the glass changes. This change in sound indicates that the glass is weakened along the score line and that the pieces can be easily broken apart.

Glass can be broken by holding the glass on one side of the scored line in breaking pliers and the other side between your fingers and thumb and twisting up and out. Or you can grip the glass on each side of the scored line between the thumb and fingers of each hand and twist your thumbs out, making the wrists and palms turn up while simultaneously pulling away from the scored line. It is difficult to grasp the glass between the fingers and thumb if the pieces are very small. In this case, hold the glass on one

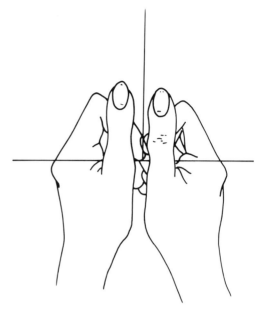

Fig 17  Grasp the scored glass along the score line between the fingers and thumbs. Snap the glass by turning wrists and palms up quickly

Use breaking or grozing pliers to break smaller pieces of glass

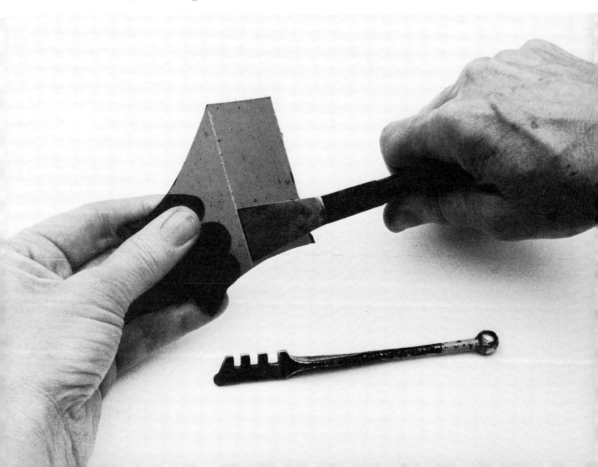

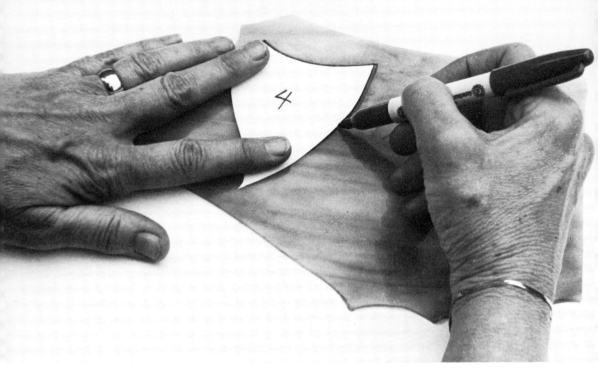

Lay each pattern piece on glass and draw around it with a glass-marking pen. Score the glass just inside the pen line

side of the scored line with breaking pliers, and place grozing or other pliers on the other side of the line. Twist the pliers up and out to break the glass.

Glass must be accurately cut for the pieces within a composition to fit together precisely. This is accomplished by laying each pattern piece on the glass and drawing around it with a glass-marking pen. Cut the glass *just inside this line.* Some people simply score around the pattern while holding it against the glass with one hand. Although this is much faster, it is not nearly as accurate and the resulting pieces are often too large. After each piece of glass is cut, place it over the cartoon to check for accuracy. If the piece does not fit the cartoon *exactly,* then you might alter the pattern of the next piece of glass to be cut to compensate for the poor fit. If the piece fits really poorly, it would be best to cut another and aim for a proper fit. Be sure to check the pattern size before cutting another piece of glass.

Before cutting expensive stained glass, it is advisable to find some old clear window glass and practise scoring and breaking until you feel comfortable with the technique. Clear glass is softer and more easily scored than stained glass; but still, the experience of practising the movements of scoring and breaking glass is invaluable for the beginner.

It is important to approach the breaking of glass with self-confidence and conviction. Halting movements and an attitude of doubt will all too often result in a poor break; a positive attitude and resolute movements are needed.

## Grinding Glass

After a piece of glass has been scored and broken and you have checked that it conforms to the shape of a pattern piece, it is helpful to grind the edges to remove snags and/or slivers and to make the edges square, ie at a right angle to the glass surface. This is particularly important if the glass is to be foiled. If you have a glass grinder that is lubricated with water, the grinding process takes very

Notice the top part of the glass-grinder head is smaller than the bottom section. This small head is used to make holes and grind sharp curves and angles that are not possible to cut by ordinary cutting procedures

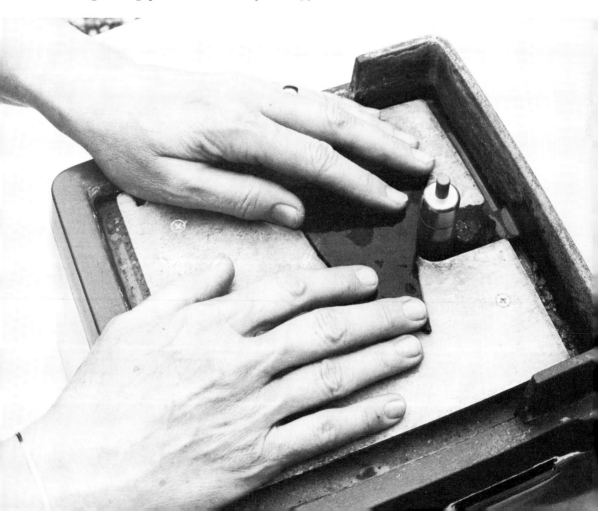

The edges of glass can also be smoothed by grinding them with a regular workbench grinder. The glass should be ground slowly because it chips if it is held too firmly against the grinding wheel. Be sure to wear protective goggles when grinding glass

little time and does not jeopardize the glass, but if you use a workshop grinder that is not lubricated with water, then it is important to hold the glass very lightly against the grinding wheel because it will chip if pressed too hard. If every edge is passed over the grinding wheel, the pieces will fit together much better, and, in fact, the glass is much safer to work with — irregular edges are a threat to your hands as the pieces are being handled. Be sure to wear protective glasses while grinding glass because flecks of glass are regularly thrown out.

## Foiling

The pieces of glass that make up foiled stained-glass projects are joined together with strips of copper foil held to the edges of the glass with an adhesive backing; solder applied to the foil holds the adjacent pieces of glass together. The sticky or adhesive side of the copper foil is

Wrap the edges of the glass in copper foil, pressing it securely against the glass

Fold the overhanging foil onto the surface of the glass and press it smooth with a flat piece of plastic or wood

Place foiled glass over the cartoon, check for proper fit, and proceed to cut the remaining pieces of glass

covered with protective paper that can be easily peeled off as the foil is applied to the edges of the glass. Carefully wrap the edges of each piece of glass in foil with the sticky side against the glass edge. Overlap the ends of the foil about 1/4in (6mm). With your finger tips, bend the protruding edges of the copper ribbon onto the glass surface. Lay the glass on a smooth surface and with the shaft of a pen, a smooth piece of wood, or a lathekin, press the foil against the glass to ensure that the sticky surface adheres to the glass, to work out little bumps, and to flatten the corners of the foil. Place the foiled glass over the cartoon and proceed to the next piece of glass.

## Leading

The alternative method of joining pieces of glass together is called leading. Pieces

Apply steady pressure on the lead knife, rocking it back and·forth until the came is severed

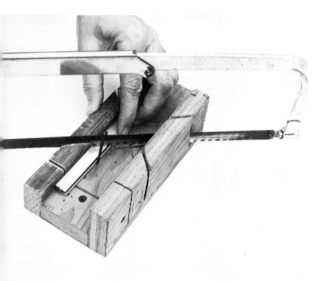

Zinc came is very sturdy and cannot be cut by the usual techniques used for lead. To cut zinc, secure it in a mitre box or vice and saw it with a hacksaw

of glass that make up windows larger than 2-2½ft (0.7-0.85m) square are usually held together with strips of lead that are placed between the pieces of glass and then soldered together where they intersect. (Smaller windows can also be leaded.)

Lead must be stretched and straightened before it is used. Lay a length of lead (6ft or 2m long) on the work table and fasten one end of it in a vice or lead clamp. Hold the other end with pliers and pull straight back firmly and evenly until the lead becomes straight and taut. A 6ft (2m) length of came should be stretched about 3in (75mm). Determine the length of each piece of lead along with the proper angles for each end — each end must be cut so it will fit snugly against the lead it intercepts. Some ends will be sharply angled while others will be square. As each piece of glass is added to the composition, fit came along its edge, working from the corner and making sure the glass is secured in the channel.

Lead is a very soft metal. It can be cut to size with a lead knife, hacksaw blade, or lead snippers. If a lead knife is used, place the knife against the came and rock it back and forth, pressing down gently to avoid distorting the shape of the came. If a hacksaw blade is used, lay the lead on a flat surface, hold it securely and saw lightly. The saw disfigures the lead less than the knife. Both methods can be used for angled or right-angled cuts, though lead snips are the best and quickest way to make right-angled cuts. If the edges are rough after cutting, carefully smooth them with a flat metal file, which will fit nicely into the groove of the lead. Fit the groove of the lead over the glass on the work board, secure it with nails driven into the building board and proceed to the next piece of glass. After lead has been placed between several pieces of glass, solder the lead together where it intersects. When you are more experienced, you can achieve a better finished result by completing the jigsaw of glass and lead before soldering. This allows you to move the glass pieces *in situ*.

50

When constructing a panel lamp or window panel, secure the glass and lead in position with nails driven into the building board

## Soldering

Strips of copper foil or the pieces of lead came around each piece of glass are held together with solder. Learning to make smooth lines over the foil or flat joints in the lead takes a little practice.

Before soldering, the tip of the iron must be 'tinned', ie covered with a thin film of solder. Put a ¼in (6mm) length of solder in a bottle cap or other shallow vessel. Brush flux onto the solder and push the hot iron into the solder, turning the iron so each side of the tip is covered. Keep a damp cloth or sponge handy to wipe the tip when extraneous materials stick to it.

Before soldering a panel, practise on a few scraps of lead so that you know how much heat is needed to make the solder flow, and that the lead can be damaged, literally melted, if the iron is too hot. On the other hand, if the iron is not hot enough, the solder will form peaks. Maintaining the iron at the proper temperature is an important key to producing smooth seams and joints. The temperature of the iron changes during soldering because heat is drained from the iron as it

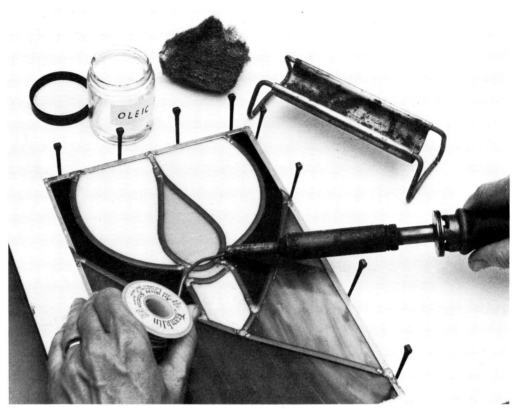

is used. For this reason, it is necessary to solder at a speed that will maintain the heat of the iron. This is not a problem if an iron of high wattage (100-150) is used, but an iron with a lower wattage is quickly drained of heat — which means stopping work while the iron reheats.

Brush flux over each seam or joint just before soldering. Flux prevents oxidation of the hot metal and assures the adhesion of the solder to the foil or lead. Apply flux to a small area at a time and solder soon afterwards.

Check the union of each lead joint before soldering. A close-fitting joint is easier to solder than if a gap must be filled. Nonetheless, sometimes gaps do exist and it is necessary to fill them with lead before soldering. To do this, flatten a short length of scrap lead came by hammering it to a thickness of about $1/32$in (0.7mm). Cut a piece of this to fill the gap. Make the patch a snug fit, otherwise it

Touch the soldering-iron tip to the joints while holding solder against the side of the iron tip

COLOUR PLATE
Shasta Daisy Lamp, with leaves (page 130)
Shasta Daisy Lamp, without leaves (page 130)

52

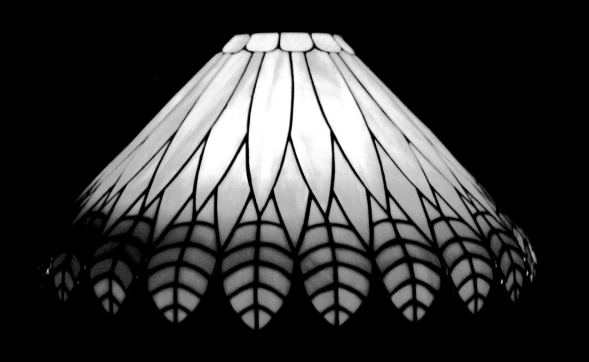

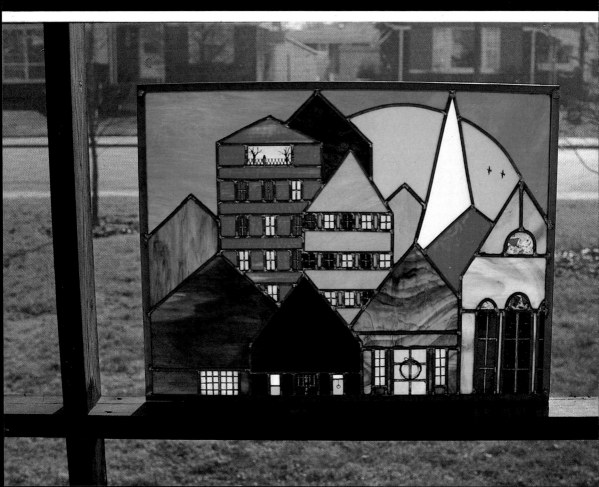

Tape foiled pieces together before tack soldering

has a tendency to move when the solder is applied.

When applying solder to lead, touch the iron to the spot to be soldered while simultaneously touching the solder to the side of the tip of the iron. Do not move the iron around, but lift it straight up from the soldered joint. After soldering, rub the joint gently with steel wool to dull the shine.

When applying solder to copper foil, touch the solder to the side of the iron tip and then move the iron along the foil line, keeping the solder on the side of the iron. The continuous flow of solder will make a smooth line. Finish each seam by 'beading', ie apply another continuous flow of solder along the solder line to give a slightly raised line or bead.

After all the joints or seams on the front are soldered, turn it over so the joints and seams on the other side can be done. Be careful! The article is very fragile at this point and may fall apart if improperly handled. If the panel is small, gently pull it to the edge of the work board and pick up the edge closest to you while supporting it with both hands. Keep the far edge resting on the table and pull it towards you as you stand the panel on its edge (see overleaf). Turn it over as you lay it down. If the panel is larger, even 2 x 2ft (0.7 x 0.7m), it will be too fragile to turn in this manner and you will need someone to help. Put a sheet of plywood over the panel, and turn it sandwiched between the plywood and the building board. Firmly squeeze the two boards together while turning. Explain to your helper exactly what is to be done *before* the turning is done. Indecision at a critical point in the turning can be disastrous. Solder each joint and seam on the back side of the panel.

When soldering the back of a copperfoiled panel, place the front on a moist cotton towel. The moist towel will absorb heat and prevent the solder melting through to the front. If that happens, you need to smooth the joints on the front side, but this is tedious because of the

a

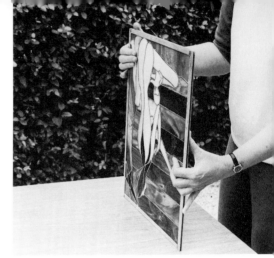

c

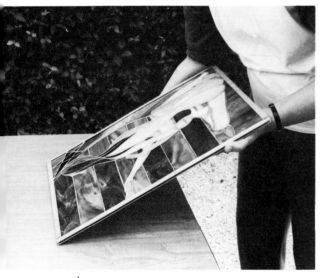

b

After soldering the joints and seams on one side, the panel must be turned over to do the other side. Turn it over as shown. The panel is very fragile at this point, and it will fall apart if not handled carefully

d

large amount of solder. It is not necessary to bead the seams on the back of a copper-foiled panel but it will add strength.

## Sealing Leaded Compositions

If lead came is used to join pieces of glass the panel must be sealed, especially if it is exposed to weather, but it is not necessary to seal foiled articles. After soldering is complete, the tiny gaps and grooves between the glass and lead must be filled with putty. This firms the glass in the lead channel and makes the panel much stronger. Sealing also prevents rattling and it waterproofs the window. The material used to seal leaded panels is a mixture of putty or glazing compound and linseed oil. Make a slurry of these two ingredients — add the linseed oil to the putty and stir until the mixture has the consistency of very thick cream and is free of lumps. Drop blobs of the grey slurry onto the panel and smear it around with a small brush (nail or scrubbing brush). Push it under the lead leaf with a circular motion. Brush in all directions. Continue to add the putty mixture until no more can be pushed under the lead. Next, sprinkle sawdust over the window and push the sawdust around (with a clean brush) to absorb the residual putty. Brush off the putty-laden sawdust and sprinkle on a fresh batch of sawdust. Remove as much residual putty as possible. Turn the window over and repeat the puttying and cleaning process. If putty drips through to the opposite side there must have been a loose fit, but the putty fills the gaps and leaves the window sealed. It is usually necessary to run along both sides of each strip of lead with a blunt pencil or knife to remove the putty that protrudes from the lead leaf. Be very

Sealing leaded compositions. Push a slurry of putty mixed with linseed oil under each piece of came, and brush vigorously in all directions

Remove excess putty with sawdust. Sprinkle sawdust over the panel, rub it around and the excess putty will adhere to it. Brush the sawdust off and repeat

careful not to gouge under the lead leaf as this may upset the seal or damage the lead.

And now a little patience is needed — you must wait at least a week before mounting a sealed panel in a frame or casing; this allows time for the putty to 'set up'. Do not putty the back of mirrored projects because the putty will damage the silvered surface.

### Cleaning Leaded Panels

Some people follow the sawdust procedure with a dusting of whiting (powdered calcium carbonate) to clean the window. Calcium carbonate is an excellent cleanser that removes oil and leaves the surface of the glass sparkling clean. However, the white powder adheres to the grey putty, making it spotted with white.

58

For this reason, I prefer a final cleaning with still another batch of sawdust, followed by a rub with a soft cloth to produce a shine.

Another good way to clean leaded lights is to rub on black cement dye ($\frac{1}{2}$ tsp per 2 sq ft [0.2 sq m]) with a medium-sized shoe brush. This cleans the glass and makes the lead and solder shiny black. Sealing and cleaning glass compositions is a tedious but very important task.

## Patina Finish for Foiled Items

A patina finish can be added to foiled items to darken the solder lines and make the item look old or weathered. The finish can be either black (purchase 'black patina' at a craft shop) or copper which is obtained by brushing on a solution of copper sulphate dissolved in water. This can also be purchased at a craft shop. The black patina reacts with some glass to make the surface dull, so apply it only to the solder lines, and quickly wipe the glass if some inadvertently gets on it. Continue to add patina finish until the desired colour is

Draw around the came carefully with a blunt pencil to remove protruding putty. It is important to hold the pencil perpendicular to the glass so as not to gouge out putty from under the lead

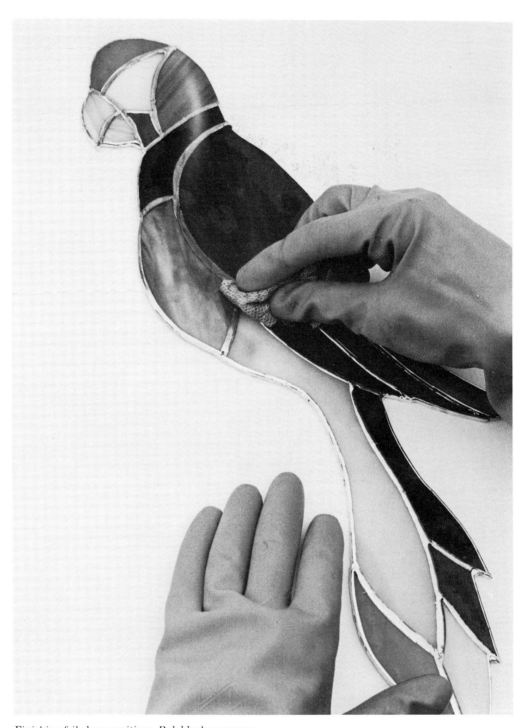

Finishing foiled compositions. Rub black or copper
patina on the solder lines to darken them. Wash im-
mediately in hot sudsy water

achieved, wiping off the solution before applying more. If the soldered seams are not adequately affected by the patina, it could be because the solder is covered with a residue. In this case, carefully rub the solder with steel wool and reapply the finish. Clean the panel by washing thoroughly with detergent and water.

As you can see, there is a lot of work to do even after the last piece of glass has been soldered in place, but each step is important to the successful completion of the project.

## Support Rods (Tie Bars)

Support rods add considerable strength and are a necessity if the window or panel is very large, or if it is located where it may be subjected to wind stress or frequently jarred as in a door. As glass and lead are heavy a panel weighs nearly 3lb per square foot (14.6kg per square metre). Thus, a window just 2 x 3ft (0.7 x 1.0m) will weigh around 18lb (8kg). Foiled windows are not as heavy as leaded ones, but if they are large they also will need support rods (otherwise known as tie bars). Sometimes the weight of the lead and glass will cause a window to sag after it has been in position for many years, so add support rods if the window is larger than 2 x 2ft (0.7 x 0.7m). The rule of thumb for the placement of rods is one horizontal support rod every 1½-2ft (45-60cm) along the vertical dimension of the window. A variety of rods is available including iron or brass rods of ¼in (6mm) diameter, and flat copper rods. Brass or copper rods can be soldered directly to the seams that intersect the horizontal line. If iron rods are used, you must solder copper wires, each about 4in (10cm) long, to the lead or foil seams which intercept the line of the iron rod. Solder the centre of each wire to the lead or foil, leaving the ends, each about 2in (50mm) long, free to twist around the support rod. If the rod spans only the window, then lay the rod over the copper wires and twist the wires around it. Do not twist too tightly as this can pull the wire from the solder. Flatten the twisted wires so they lay flat against the support rod.

A rod will give much better support if it extends into the window frame. I prefer to use rods attached with copper wires rather than copper or brass rods soldered to the panel, because the former can more readily be set into the window frame and can more easily be removed if the window is to be transferred to another location. To extend the support rods into the frame, place the stained-glass panel, with the wires soldered in position, into the window opening and mark the frame where holes for the rods should be drilled. These should be in line with the wires to be twisted around the support rods. Remove the window and drill holes in the frame. The rod should be about 2in (50mm) longer than the window is wide. Therefore, the hole on one side of the window should be 2in (50mm) deep so the rod can be put into position, and the hole on the other side of the frame should be 1in (25mm) deep. Return the stained-glass window to the opening, put the rod in place and twist the copper wires around the support rods. Clip off excess wire and press the twisted wire flat against the rod.

Many stained-glass windows are small and require no support rods. If a small window is to be installed where a clear window already exists, the clear glass can remain in position and the art glass can be installed inside it. In fact, it is sometimes preferable to install clear glass outside to protect the stained glass and act as insulation. If the art-glass window requires support rods and the already existing clear glass is difficult to remove, then support rods for the stained glass can be installed on the inside. Surprisingly, rods do not interfere with the beauty of a window because the eye looks past them and they are lost in the design.

Windows that face onto busy streets can be protected with a plexiglass covering. One rock strategically aimed can cause a lot of heartache for the owner of a beautiful window, so it's only wise to prevent this from happening by installing a protective covering.

Sometimes art-glass windows should not be installed permanently — you may want them to be passed from generation to generation and cherished. This is especially true of windows that were made by a member of the family, or a window that has a family heirloom incorporated into it. You should consider how long you plan to remain in your home, and, if you move frequently, you might prefer to install art-glass windows so they can be easily moved. Perhaps the simplest way to install a window temporarily is to place it in a wooden frame with substantial hooks at the top of the frame. Then the art glass can be hung with decorative chains or macrame cords to the inside of an already existing window. This technique is especially useful in apartment buildings where alterations are frowned upon.

Stained-glass windows can be 'framed' with a false wall and then placed in front of a window. Curtains cover the false wall, and the shape of the original window is obscured, allowing you to reshape it. This decorating trick can also be used to create a window where none exists. A stained-glass panel framed with curtains and lit from behind with fluorescent tubes can be a clever way of brightening up a plain wall that has no window.

# 5  Suncatchers

The best way to start working with stained glass is to make suncatchers. For very little expense and a minimum of time and effort, a beginner can produce delightful objects to hang in windows, and in the process learn some of the techniques that lead to more sophisticated stained-glass work.

Suncatchers can be made from previously formed glass pieces called globs or nuggets, or they can be made of glass that is cut to fit a pattern. Glass nuggets are shaped like small biscuits — flat on one side and rounded on the other. They come in various sizes and colours and are very effective in suncatchers because they catch and reflect the sun's rays in interesting ways. They are a special pleasure for the beginner to work with because they require no glass cutting.

However, most suncatchers will require pieces of glass cut to fit the shape of a pattern. Since these are usually small pieces, it is advisable to cut them from scrap glass. Scrap glass can be purchased at most stained-glass suppliers for a much lower price than large sheets of glass. The glass in suncatchers can be held together by either the foil or lead methods described in Chapter 4.

Suncatchers sell well. If you are just getting into stained-glass craft, you might enjoy making a batch of suncatchers for a craft show or bazaar. Simplicity is the key to commercial success — pretty, charming objects, which are made and sold inexpensively, will attract buyers.

The suncatcher patterns in this book are designed for beginners. The first five can be made completely of glass nuggets with no cut glass, while others require simple glass cutting. Wire is an integral part of many of them — use iron or copper, but not aluminium wire because solder will not adhere to it. Begin with the easiest patterns early in the chapter and work towards the more difficult ones. Instructions are very detailed in the first projects, but, to avoid repetition, these details are increasingly omitted.

## Kermit the Frog

*Project complexity: 1*
Glass nuggets
Wire
Foil (¼in) or U-channel lead (⅛in)

Fig 18  Kermit the Frog

A large 1½in (38mm) green nugget is used for the frog's body. The eyes can be either green or yellow ¾in (20mm) nuggets, and the silly grin is simply a piece of wire strategically placed and soldered in position. The legs and feet are also made of wire.

Wrap the glass nuggets in copper foil, firmly pressing the sticky side of the foil against the glass. Cover the foil with solder and then attach the eyes to the body with drops of solder. Alternatively, cut the lead so it wraps around each nugget exactly, and solder the ends of the lead where they meet. Position the eyes so they touch the body where the lead joins, then secure them to the body with a drop of solder. Finally, solder a piece of wire between the eyes (to attach a wire or thread for hanging), a piece of wire for the mouth, and a piece of bent wire for each of the legs.

## Wise Owl

*Project complexity: 1*

Glass nuggets
Wire or lead
Copper foil (¼in) or U-channel lead (⅛in)

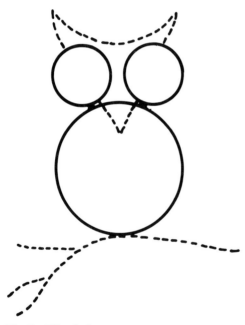

Fig 19   Wise Owl

The body of this little owl should be made of a 1½in (38mm) amber nugget, and the eyes might be red, green, or yellow ¾in (20mm) nuggets. The ears and beak can be wire or lead. The branch is wire, or, if you prefer, it can be a real twig with wire twisted around it so it can be soldered to the owl.

Wrap the nuggets in foil or lead. If foil is used, cover it with solder. If lead is used, solder the ends where they meet. Attach the eyes to the body with drops of solder. The ears and beak can be cut from lead or they can be made of wire and soldered in position.

If wire is used for the twig, twist several pieces together. Use two pairs of pliers to hold the wire while twisting, and separate the wires to create a branching pattern.

You can make an owl pendant by using smaller nuggets — and make the twig from wire.

## Charlotte and Her Web

*Project complexity: 1*

Glass nuggets
Wire
Foil (¼in) or U-channel lead (⅛in)

The spider is composed of two leaded or foiled nuggets. Use any colour ¾in (20mm) nugget for the head, and a 1½in (38mm) nugget for the body. The eyes are drops of solder and the legs are wire. The web is also made of wire and soldered together. It is helpful to hold the pieces of wire in position with tweezers or forceps while soldering them together. The spider is soldered to the web at the tip of each of its eight legs.

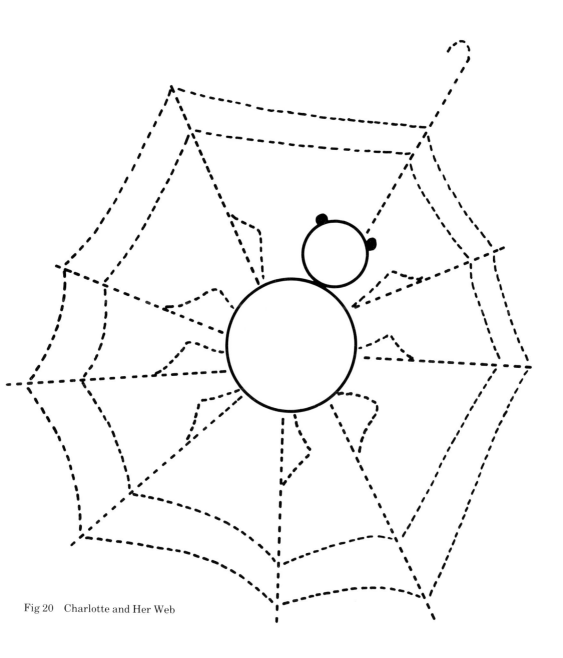

Fig 20   Charlotte and Her Web

65

## Musical Notes

*Project complexity: 1*

Glass nuggets
Wire
Foil (¼in) or U-channel lead (⅛in)

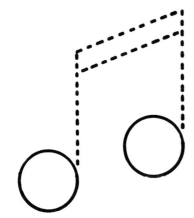

Fig 21   Musical Notes

Simple! Surround two nuggets with foil or U-came. Wires form the stems of the notes, and wires or a piece of lead make the two cross-pieces. Attach a hanging loop to the top cross-piece, positioned so the notes will hang correctly.

It's surprising how many people are associated with musical groups — a band, orchestra, or choir — and this little suncatcher is a perfect gift for them.

## A Tree for All Seasons

*Project complexity: 1*

16 glass nuggets (¾in or 20mm)
U-channel lead (⅛in)

This single design can be used to depict the four seasons as well as a Christmas tree. The tree is composed of glass nuggets wrapped in U-channel lead came and contains no cut pieces of glass. Use the following colours for seasonal variations.

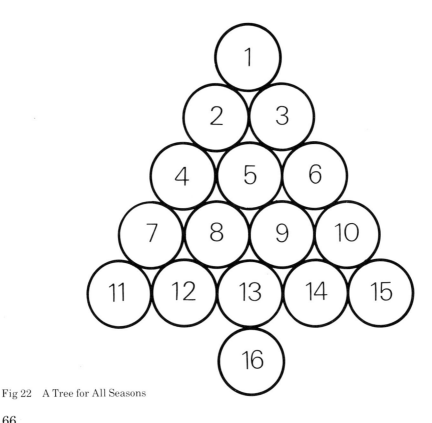

Fig 22   A Tree for All Seasons

*Winter tree* Pieces 1, 2, 3, and 4 are white nuggets, 16 is brown, and the remaining ones are dark green.

*Spring tree* Pieces 2, 6, and 8 are pink or light violet, 16 is brown, and the remaining pieces are light green.

*Summer tree* Make 2, 6, and 8 red to represent apples, 16 is brown, and the remaining pieces are dark green.

*Autumn tree* Use a mixture of yellow, orange, amber, and brown nuggets for the tree. Number 16 is brown.

The summer tree can also be used as a Christmas tree. A single red nugget in position 9, with the remaining ones green, is another idea for a Christmas tree.

Wrap each nugget in U-channel lead, cut so it wraps exactly around each piece. Solder where the lead ends meet. Place all the pieces in position and attach them together with strategically placed drops of solder. Turn over and solder the joints on the back. Add a tiny loop of wire at the top of the tree for hanging.

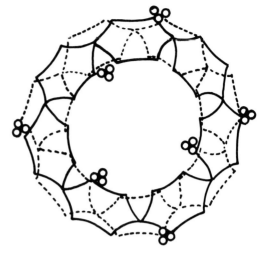

Fig 23    Holly Wreath assembly

## Holly Wreath or Holly Sprig

*Project complexity: 2*

Wreath: 14 pieces of green cut glass; 21 red glass nuggets (½in or 12mm)

Holly sprig: 3 pieces of green cut glass; 3 red nuggets (½in or 12mm)

Foil (¼in)

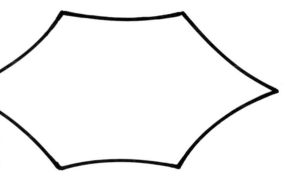

Fig 24    Cartoon for leaf pattern

Cut fourteen holly leaves from two shades of green cathedral or green opalescent glass. Foil the leaves and cover the foil with solder. Place seven leaves, with the tips of the leaves touching, in a circle. The circle will be about 8in (20cm) in diameter. Place the remaining seven leaves on top of the first seven, positioning them so the ends of the top leaves are over the centres of the bottom ones (see illustration). Solder the leaves together at each place where the foiled edges touch. Intersperse the red foiled nuggets, in units of three, among the leaves to represent berries.

A holly sprig can be made with three leaves and three nuggets as shown in the illustration.

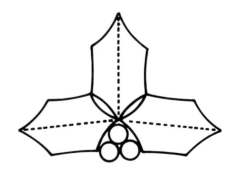

Fig 24a    Sprig assembly

## Candle in Holder

*Project complexity: 1+*

3 pieces of cut glass
Foil (¼in)
Wire

Just three pieces of cut glass make this
lovely piece. The flame should be yellow
opalescent, the candle white or red, and
the holder any colour you choose. Use
wire to form the candle-holder handle.
Allow solder to flow down the candle from
the foil, to make the realistic 'wax'.

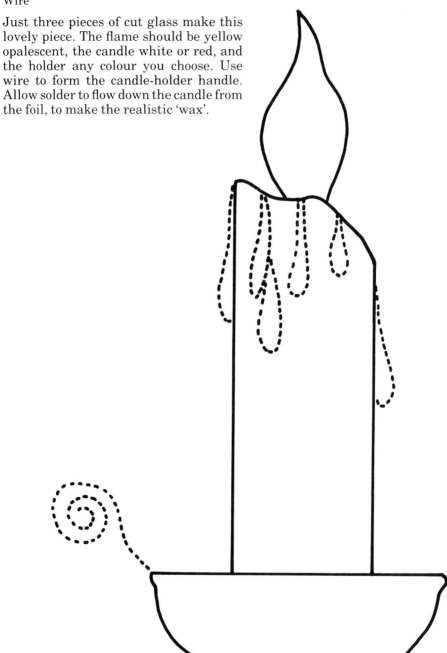

Fig 25   Candle in Holder

## Wedding or Christmas Bells

*Project complexity: 2*

8 pieces of cut glass and 3 glass nuggets
Foil (1/4in)

The colours used determine whether these will be wedding or Christmas bells. Wedding bells should be white, with gold ribbon and clappers of amber nuggets. Christmas bells should be white with a red ribbon and green clappers.

Fig 26   Wedding or Christmas Bells

69

## Tulip

*Project complexity: 2+*

8 pieces of cut glass
Foil (¼in)

The flower can be any pale opalescent — yellow is attractive. The leaves and stem should be green opalescent, two shades if available. The shaded areas are left open.

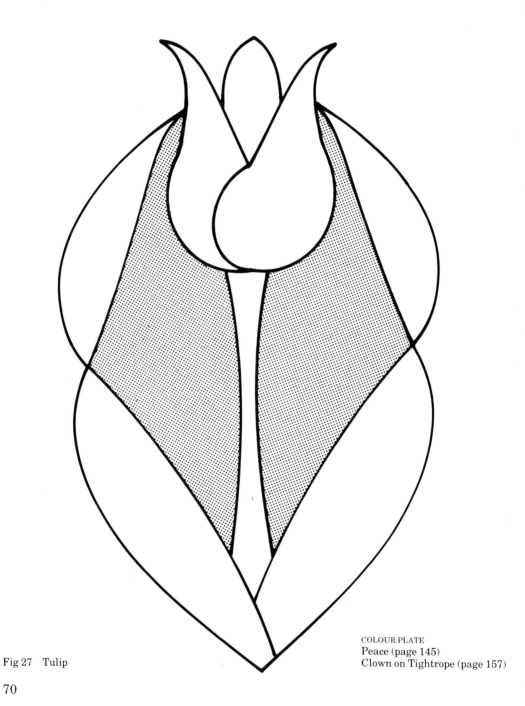

Fig 27  Tulip

COLOUR PLATE
Peace (page 145)
Clown on Tightrope (page 157)

## Cardinal

*Project complexity: 3*

11 pieces of cut glass
Wire
Foil (¼in)

Use red cathedral for pieces 1 to 5; black opaque for 6; yellow opalescent for 7; orange or yellow opalescent for 8; and green opalescent for 9, 10, and 11. Divide the bill into two parts with a wire. The stem is made of two or three wires twisted together and then soldered to the bird — or a natural twig wrapped in foil and soldered to the bird and leaves.

COLOUR PLATE
Harlequin (page 158)

Fig 28   Cardinal

## Cluster of Grapes

*Project complexity: 2*

14 nuggets (¾in or 20mm)
3 pieces of cut glass
Wire
Foil (¼in) or U-channel lead (⅛in)

The leaves and stem are cut glass. Make the stem either brown, amber, or green, and make the leaves green opalescent glass. Each leaf can be made of one or two pieces of glass. If each leaf is a single piece of glass the centre vein can be represented by a piece of wire. Wrap the leaves and stem in foil or lead. Use purple and violet glass nuggets for the grapes. Wrap each nugget in U-channel lead came, arrange as illustrated, or in another pleasing pattern, and solder together. Tendrils can be made from wire curled around a pencil and soldered in position.

Fig 29   Cluster of Grapes

74

## Apple, Apricot, or Plum

*Project complexity: 1+*

3 pieces of cut glass
1 glass nugget (1½in or 38mm)
Foil (¼in) and U-channel lead (⅛in)

The type of fruit is determined by the colour of the glass nugget; red for an apple, orange for an apricot or peach, and purple for a plum. Wrap the glass nugget in U-channel lead came, and solder the ends together. Cut the stem from brown or amber glass and the leaves from green opalescent. Wrap in foil or lead and solder together.

Fig 30   Apple, Apricot, or Plum

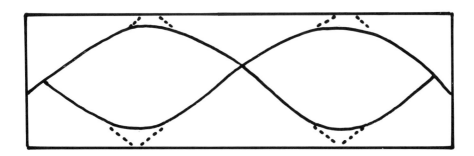

Fig 31   Leaves: cut along the solid lines and score the dotted lines to facilitate breaking the glass

**Additional Suncatcher Patterns**

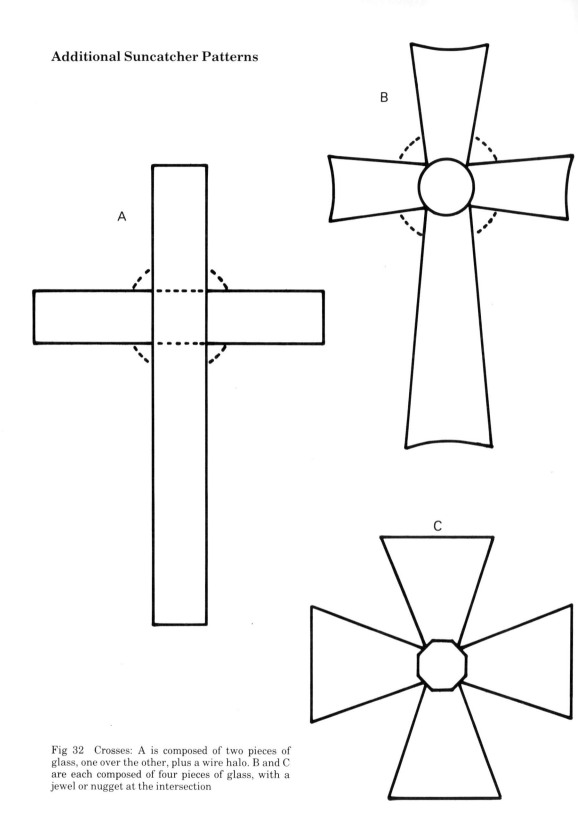

Fig 32 Crosses: A is composed of two pieces of glass, one over the other, plus a wire halo. B and C are each composed of four pieces of glass, with a jewel or nugget at the intersection

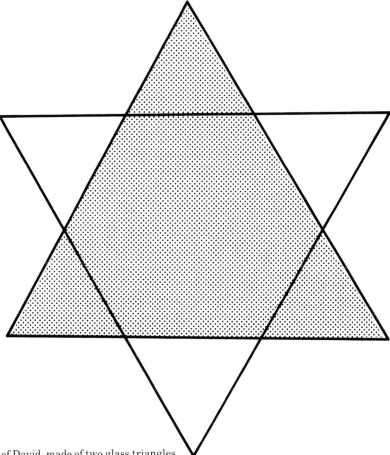

Fig 33   Star of David, made of two glass triangles,
one over the other

Fig 34   Red Rover. The shaded areas contain no
glass; the wheels are made of nuggets or cut glass

Fig 35   Cat on Fence. Use nuggets or cut glass for
the head and body; wire for the whiskers

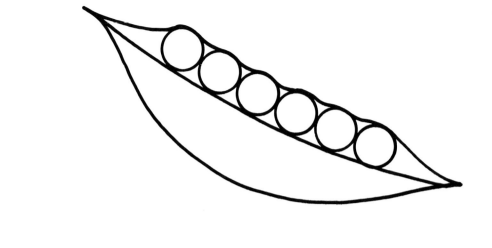

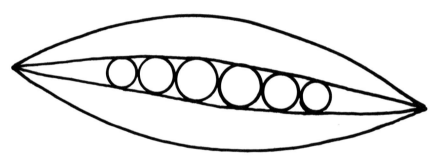

Fig 36  Pea Pods. Use green nuggets to represent
peas, leaving the areas between the peas and pods
empty

Fig 37 Rose Bud. Make the thorns from flattened pieces of lead

Fig 38 Iris. Leave shaded areas open

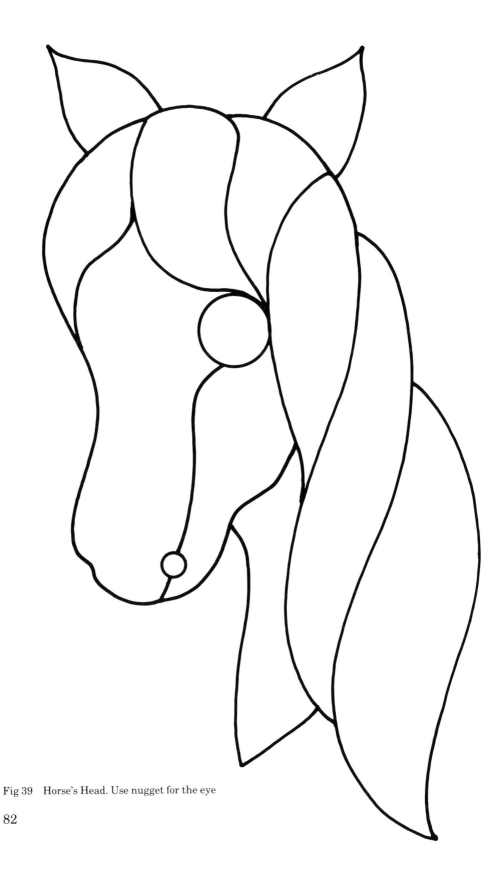

Fig 39  Horse's Head. Use nugget for the eye

82

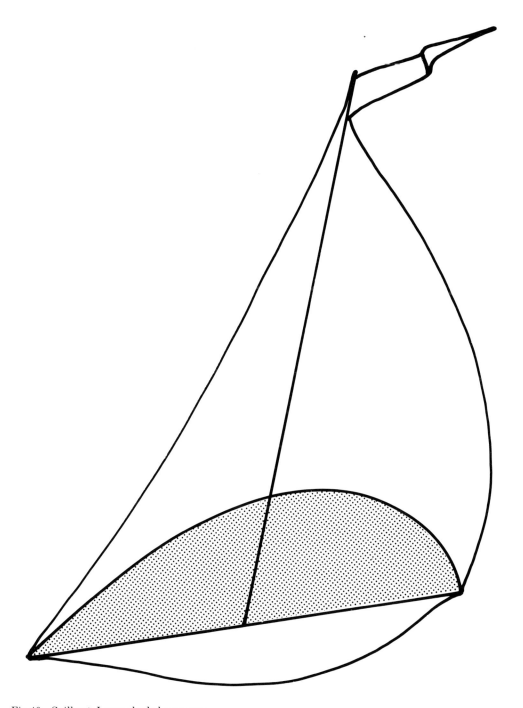

Fig 40   Sailboat. Leave shaded area open

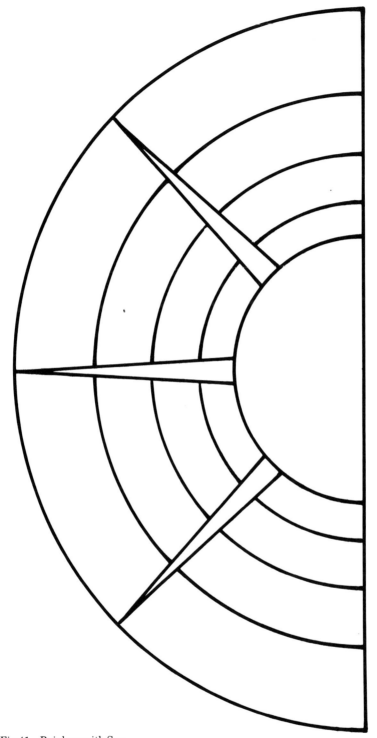

Fig 41   Rainbow with Sun

84

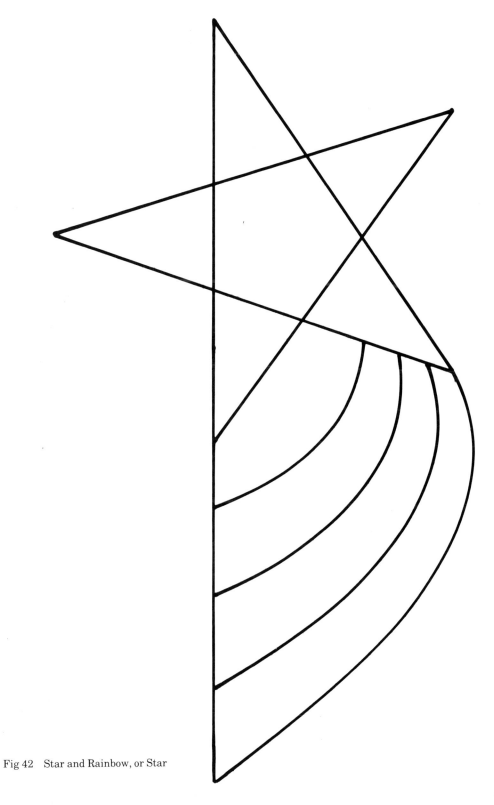

Fig 42   Star and Rainbow, or Star

Fig 43 Clown. Use nuggets for nose and top of hat and wire for ruffle on hat. Paint eyes with oil or acrylic paint

86

# 6 Frames, Mirrors, Mobiles, etc

The projects in this section illustrate the diverse ways stained glass can be used to make a variety of articles, other than windows. The same techniques used to create stained-glass items can also be used to make mirrored compositions, and several mirrored projects are included.

## Picture or Mirror Frame

*Project complexity: 2*
*Assembly technique: foil*
*Composed of 15 pieces of glass*
*Enlarge to desired size*

These materials will make a frame for a 5 x 7in (12 x 17cm) photograph or mirror.

*Glass:*
6 x 12in (15 x 30cm) green opalescent, two shades
Flower: 4 x 5in (10 x 12cm) contrasting pastel opalescent (pink, yellow or purple)
5 x 7in (12 x 17cm) clear glass or mirror (single strength)

60/40 solder and flux
Copper foil (¼in or narrower)

1 Using the grid method described in Chapter 4, enlarge the design to the desired size. This should be done on sturdy kraft paper or brown paper as this will serve as the cartoon over which the frame will be constructed.
2 Make a copy of the cartoon on thin poster paper. Cut this copy apart and use the pieces for the pattern.
3 Lay each pattern piece on the stained glass and draw around it with a glass-marking pen.
4 Cut the glass, grind the edges if necessary and foil each piece. Place each piece in position over the cartoon.
5 When all the pieces are in position, solder them together, and then lay a bead of solder along each seam on the front.

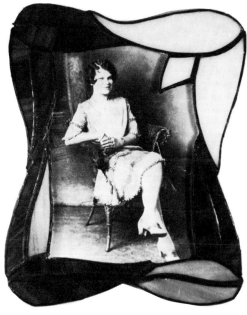

Stained-glass picture frame

Cover the foiled edge of the frame with solder.
6 Cut and foil clear glass or mirror and solder it to the back of the frame. Add wire loops for hanging.

87

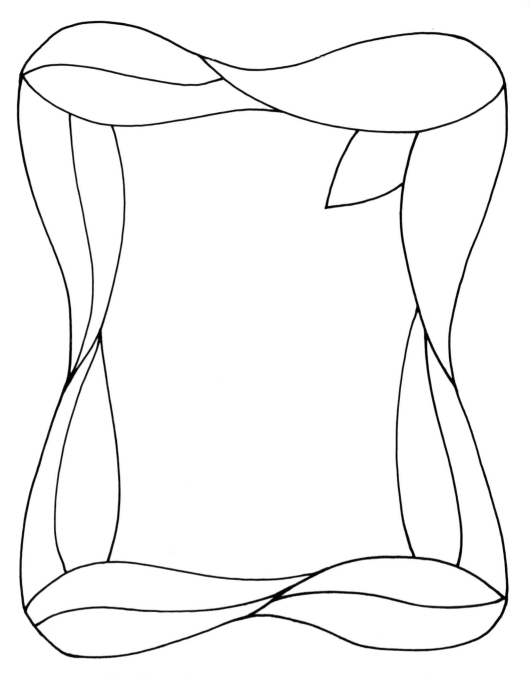

Fig 44    Picture or Mirror Frame cartoon

## Terrarium or Tissue Box

*Project complexity: 4*
*Assembly technique: foil*
*Composed of 53 pieces of glass*
*Reduced cartoon (overleaf)*

This container may be used as either a terrarium or a tissue box. It is essential to make the corners square. Therefore, before beginning work, nail strips of wood to your work board at a 90 degree angle, and construct the sides of the box against these wood strips. These materials will make a box 10½in (26cm) long (see page 92).

*Glass*
Bottom, sides and front: 2sq ft (0.2sq m) clear or opalescent
Windows and sun design: ¼sq ft (0.025sq m) yellow opalescent
Door: 3 x 4in (7.5 x 10cm) opalescent or cathedral (your choice of colour)
Roof: ½sq ft (0.05sq m) your choice

60/40 solder and flux
Copper foil (¼in)

1 On light poster paper make two carbon copies of the cartoon for the *ends* of the terrarium. Number the pieces and cut apart one of the copies to use for the pattern, cutting off the pencil lines between the pieces. This narrow pencil line is the amount of space taken by the foil that will be placed around the glass. The ends will be constructed over the remaining copy of the cartoon. Next, enlarge the side panel design, make a carbon copy and cut apart for use as pattern pieces.

2 Make two sides and two end panels. Lay each pattern piece on glass, draw round it with a glass-marking pen, and cut the glass just *inside* the pen line. Wrap foil round each piece of glass. The mullions of the windows and door are made of narrow strips of foil, positioned before placing the glass on the cartoon. Spot solder the pieces of glass together as the panel progresses. After the pieces of a panel are in position, cover the decorative foil on windows and door with solder and add a bead of solder to each seam on both sides.

3 After the four sides are complete, solder them together at the corners as shown in the illustration, filling the corner grooves with solder.

4 To determine the size of the bottom glass, set the joined sides and ends over a piece of glass and draw around the *inside* of the box with a glass-marking pen. Cut the glass *on the line*. Foil and solder into position.

5 Each side of the roof is composed of four pieces of glass. For each side, cut two strips of glass 1in (25mm) wide and long enough to extend from one gable to the other (nearly 10¼in [26cm]). Foil and solder the top strip in position as shown. Cut two end pieces 1 x 4¼in (25 x 107mm), foil and solder as shown, and finally solder the lower strip in place. The end and lower strips of glass make the roof overhang. Run a reinforcing bead along the line where the side wall meets the roof. If too much space exists between the junction of the side and roof, place a strip of copper foil between them and then solder. When both sides of the roof are soldered in place, fill the groove along the crest of the roof with solder.

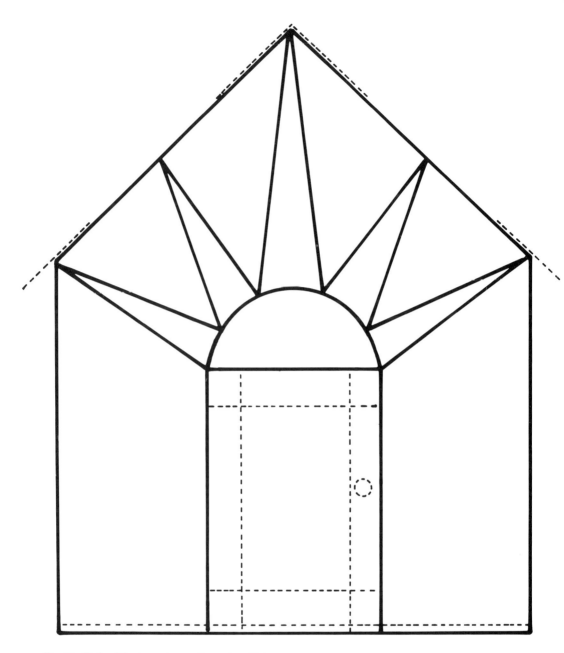

Fig 45   Ends of the terrarium or tissue box. Cut on
solid lines. Dotted lines indicate the positions of the
floor and long roof pieces. Dotted lines on the door
represent decorative foil. The door handle is a
washer, nail head, or large drop of solder

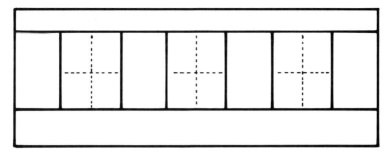

Fig 46   Design for side walls. Enlarge to 10¼ x
3¾in (261 x 95mm). Make window bars from thin
strips of foil, covered with solder

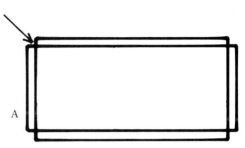

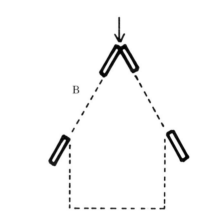

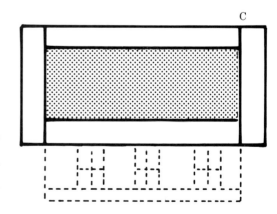

Fig 47   Assembling the terrarium or tissue box
A   Join sides and ends as shown from above, filling
the corners with solder as arrowed
B   Position the long roof pieces as shown from the
end, filling the top roof ridge with solder
C   Roof viewed from the side; the shaded area is
left open

91

Stained-glass tissue box (or terrarium)

## Mobile

*Project complexity: 2*
*Assembly technique: foil and wire*
*Composed of 20 to 35 pieces of glass*
*Full-size cartoon*

A stained-glass mobile is a unique way of putting colour and movement into an area. This one can be made with birds or angels.

Variety of scrap glass of different colours
60/40 solder and flux
Copper foil (¼in)
Wire for hanging (clothes-hanger thickness)

1 Select one cartoon out of the two given — angel or bird. Make a copy of it and cut it apart to use as the pattern.
2 Cut and foil five hanging objects (angels or birds). Position a wire loop so that the object hangs properly, and solder.

3 Create a sturdy-wire framework for hanging the glass (see Fig 50). Cut three pieces of wire, each at least 15in (38cm) long. Bend two of them in a graceful curve and bend a hook on each end. Leave the remaining wire straight except for a hook on each end. Fix two wire loops along the straight wire, slip the curved wires through them and fix so they cannot slip. Hang the glass on the framework as shown.

92

Fig 48 Angel for the mobile. Make the dress white, the wings yellow and the head from an orange or amber nugget. Solder a wire halo around the head

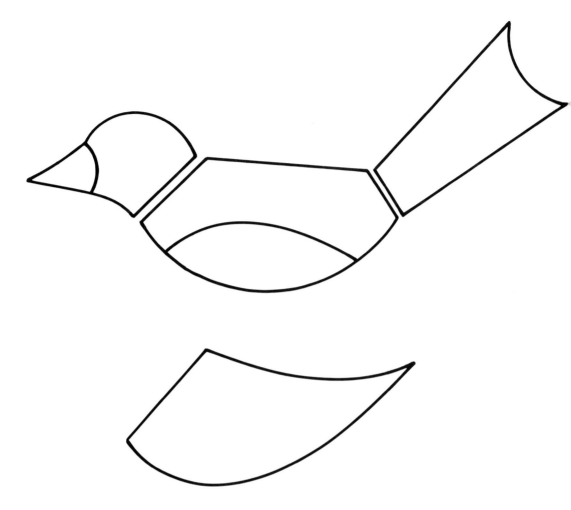

Fig 49   Bird for the mobile. Cut two wings per bird
and arrange them in any of the illustrated positions

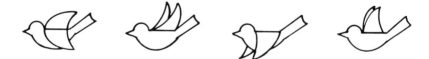

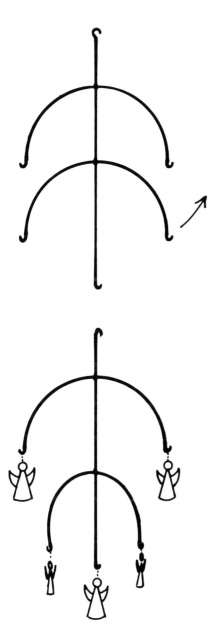

Fig 50   Make a wire suspension and hang the glass objects as shown to make the mobile

## Three-dimensional Woodpecker on Wood

*Project complexity: 3*
*Assembly technique: foil and lead*
*Composed of 27 pieces of glass*
*Reduced cartoon*

An unusual and attractive combination of glass and wood. These materials will make a 15in (38cm) long woodpecker — the size of my original and larger than the cartoon (overleaf).

*Glass*
6 x 12in (15 x 30cm) dark cathedral, black or
   purple
4 x 5in (10 x 12cm) white opalescent
1 x 2in (25 x 50mm) yellow opalescent
2 x 2in (50 x 50mm) red cathedral
yellow, blue or green marble (¼in or 6mm)
4ft (1.3m) copper wire (22 or 24 gauge) for foot
   and leg
5 x 18in (12 x 45cm) weathered barn wood or
   driftwood

60/40 solder and flux
Copper foil (¼in)
6ft (2m) U-channel came (⅛in)

This design is three dimensional — the wings are attached to the sides of the body and the marble eye protrudes from both sides of the head.
1 Enlarge the cartoon to the desired size using the grid method described in Chapter 4.
2 Make a copy of the enlarged cartoon on poster paper. Because the cartoon is a two-dimensional drawing of a three-dimensional object, you must copy the body and the wings separately. The wings are drawn over the body with dashed lines. Cut out the pieces for the pattern.
3 Place the pattern pieces on glass, draw round them and cut just inside the line. Cut and foil the pieces of each wing, lay them over the cartoon and solder them together. The marble eye has a strip of copper foil around its circumference which is then soldered in position. Cut and foil the head and body pieces and lay them over the cartoon, making certain that the eye will fit into the opening. Solder together.

95

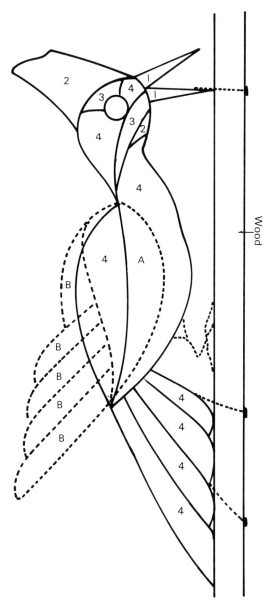

Place a bead of solder along each solder line on both sides. Next, place came around the edge of the bird, cutting the lead as needed to make the sharp angles. Place lead around the wing edges, except on the feather tips. Solder the wings to the body as shown, but at different angles.

4 If you wish to add a leg and foot, twist together twelve 22 or 24-gauge copper wires, each 4in (10cm) long. Separate the wires to make four toes, each of three twisted wires. Solder in position.

5 A copper patina can be applied to the solder lines if desired. Either mix a little copper sulphate in water or buy a copper finish at a craft shop.

6 Attach the bird to the wood. Solder a 5in (12cm) wire to the tip of the bill and similar lengths to two places on the tail, as shown. Position the bird on the board and drill holes in the wood where the wires will pass through. Pull the wires through the holes and fasten them securely to the back of the wood with staples or nails.

Fig 51 Three-dimensional Woodpecker on Wood (colour photograph page 17). The wings (shown by a dotted line) must be copied separately from the body

Fig 52 Twist copper wires to make legs and feet

*Body*
1 Yellow opalescent
2 Red cathedral
3 White opalescent
4 Dark purple or black
*Wings*
A White opalescent
B Dark purple or black cathedral

COLOUR PLATE
Janet (page 161)
*(overleaf)* Metamorphosis (page 159)

## Ice Cream Cone

*Project complexity: 4*
*Assembly technique: foil or lead*
*Composed of 20 pieces of glass*
*Reduced cartoon*

If this piece is to be a wall hanging, use only opalescent glass, but cathedral glass may be used if it will be displayed in a window. It can be used to make a large cone or a small suncatcher. The original is 15 x 36in (38 x 90cm), but the size will depend on the glass available (over) for the ice cream — swirl opalescent looks most realistic. The design can be enlarged using the grid method described in Chapter 4. The materials below will make a cone 18in (45cm) long.

*Glass*
Ice cream: 10 x 10in (25 x 25cm)swirl
    opalescent
Cone: 12 x 12in (30 x 30cm) tan or caramel
    opalescent
Cherry: 3 x 4in (7.5 x 10cm)
10in (25cm) wire (clothes-hanger thickness)
18in (45cm) flat metal strap or 12in (30cm)
    H-channel zinc came (½in)

60/40 solder and flux
10ft (3.5m) copper foil (¼in) or H-channel
    lead came (¼in)

1 Enlarge the design to the desired size and make a copy of the cartoon to use for pattern pieces.
2 Cut glass to fit each pattern piece.
3 Foil each piece of glass, or place lead came between them. The line between the ice cream and the cone is structurally weak and will require additional support. Place ½in H-Channel zinc came along this line. Alternatively, use regular lead came (or foil if appropriate) and add a vertical support rod behind the composition after it is soldered together.
4 Solder a heavy wire to the cherry and bend it to represent the stem.

Fig 53 Cartoon

COLOUR PLATE
Tommy (page 162)

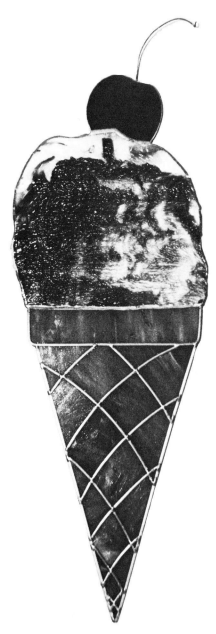

## Three-dimensional Butterfly

*Project complexity: 3*
*Assembly technique: foil or lead*
*Composed of 11 pieces of glass*
*Reduced cartoon*

This butterfly is quite simple to make —
if you bend the wings up from the body it
becomes three-dimensional. It can be displayed sitting on a piece of driftwood or
mounted on the edge of a shelf or cabinet.

Enlarge the cartoon by the grid method
in Chapter 4. Use a large glass nugget for
the head and small nuggets for the tips of
the tail. The remaining wing pieces and
the body are cut from glass. Six wire legs
can be soldered to the underside of the
body if desired.

Ice Cream Cone

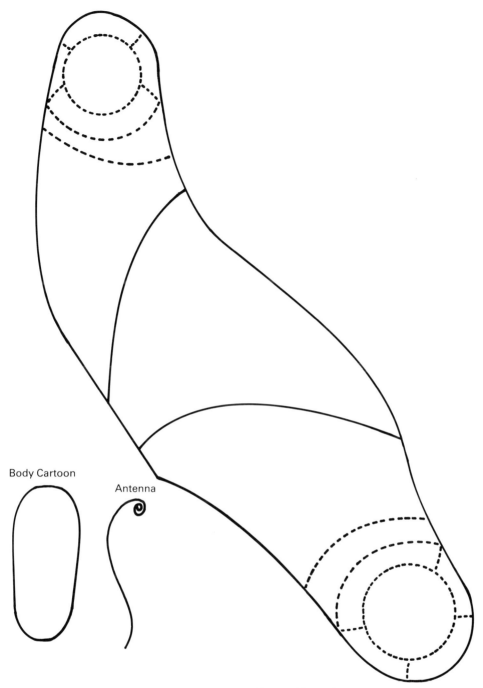

**Body Cartoon**

**Antenna**

Fig 54  Three-dimensional Butterfly. Cartoon for
wing and body, plus guide for wire antennae. Cut
two wings, turning the pattern over before cutting
the second. Cut the wings into smaller units
(dashed lines), if you feel adventurous. Use nuggets
for head and tail

103

## Free-hanging Butterfly

*Project complexity: 8*
*Assembly technique: foil and lead*
*Composed of 137 pieces of glass*
*Reduced cartoon*

This magnificent butterfly can be made with a wingspan as large as 30in (76cm) or as small as 15in (38cm). The former yields a dramatic imposing piece of art, but a smaller size is more practical. If you choose the latter, you could eliminate a few of the lines, taking out the smallest pieces. This must be done very discreetly so the design remains intact. The materials below will make a butterfly with a 30in (76cm) wingspan, which is the size of the original. Each type of glass is numbered to correspond with the numbers on the cartoon.

*Glass*
1: 2sq ft (0.2sq m) dark brown cathedral
2: 2sq ft (0.2sq m) yellow, orange, blue, or purple opalescent
3: ½sq ft (0.05 sq m) black opaque
4: ¼sq ft (0.025sq m) bright cathedral compatible with other wing colours
5: ½sq ft (0.05sq m) white opalescent
6: ⅛sq ft (0.012sq m) contrasting cathedral
7: ⅛sq ft (0.012sq m) amber cathedral
Body and head: ¼sq ft (0.025sq m) opalescent (your choice)
1½sq ft (0.15sq m) clear glass
Eyes: glass nuggets (¾in or 20mm)

60/40 solder and flux
16ft (5m) H-shaped lead came (¼in)

1 Enlarge the cartoon to the required size using the grid method described in Chapter 4.
2 On light poster paper make a carbon copy of your enlarged cartoon. Number the pieces and cut them apart for the pattern, cutting away the lines between the pieces.
3 Lay each pattern piece on glass and, with a glass-marking pen, draw around the pattern. Cut just inside the line.
4 Foil each piece of glass and place it over the cartoon. Tack or spot solder the pieces together as the work progresses. Solder the body together and place a bead of solder over each seam on both sides. Then proceed with the forewings and finally the hindwings. To ensure that the forewings match, cut each piece with its counterpart on the opposite side, building up the two wings simultaneously. Repeat with the hindwings. Continue to tack solder as the work progresses. When all pieces of a unit are in place solder them together, then turn over and solder the back. Finish by laying a bead of solder over all the seams on both sides.
5 Now solder the wings to the body. The antennae will be added in step 7.
6 Using H-shaped came (not U), surround the wings and head, cutting the lead at points indicated in Fig 56. Solder the lead came to the soldered foil where they intercept.
7 The antennae serve an additional function of supporting the large fragile wings. This is done by filling the intervening area with clear glass. Lay the antenna pattern in place and check for fit altering it if necessary. Cut the glass, fit it into the lead came at the top of the wings and place came around the remaining edges. Finally, add the antenna tips and solder in position.
8 If your butterfly has a wingspan of 20in (50cm) or more it will be necessary to add a support rod. Strike a line across the back of the butterfly as shown, and solder a copper wire to each solder seam that intersects the line. Each copper wire should be 4in (10cm) long and soldered at its centre so the ends are free. Cut a length of ¼in (6mm) iron rod to fit the wingspan across the line and twist the copper wires around the rod. Finally, solder two small wire loops to the tops of the wings, as shown.
   As an alternative, a support rod of copper can be soldered directly to the butterfly. In this case, no wires are needed.
9 A large butterfly is quite heavy and must be hung with two lengths of substantial picture-hanging wire. Run wire through each loop, then under and around the support rod. Twist each wire securely. If the butterfly is to be hung

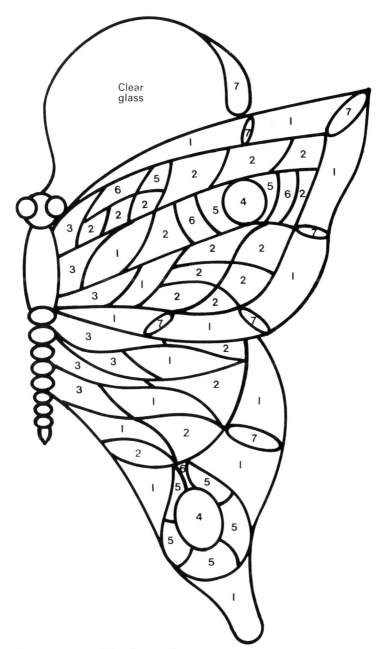

Clear
glass

from the ceiling, use two of the decorative ceiling hooks that are commonly used for hanging plants and lamps. Place each hook directly above one of the wire loops.

Fig 55 Free-hanging Butterfly (colour photograph page 18)

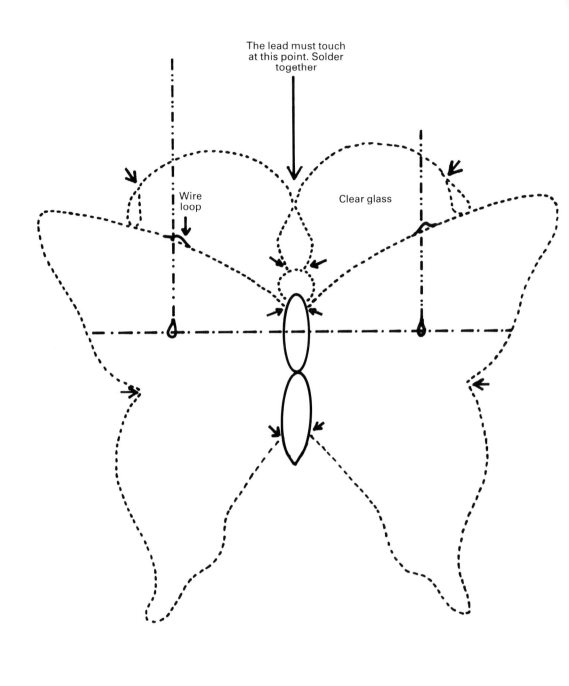

The lead must touch
at this point. Solder
together

Wire
loop

Clear glass

-------- Position of lead came
—·—·— Position of support rod
··—··— Position of hanging wire
———→ Points where the came is cut

Fig 56  Assembly guide for Free-hanging Butterfly

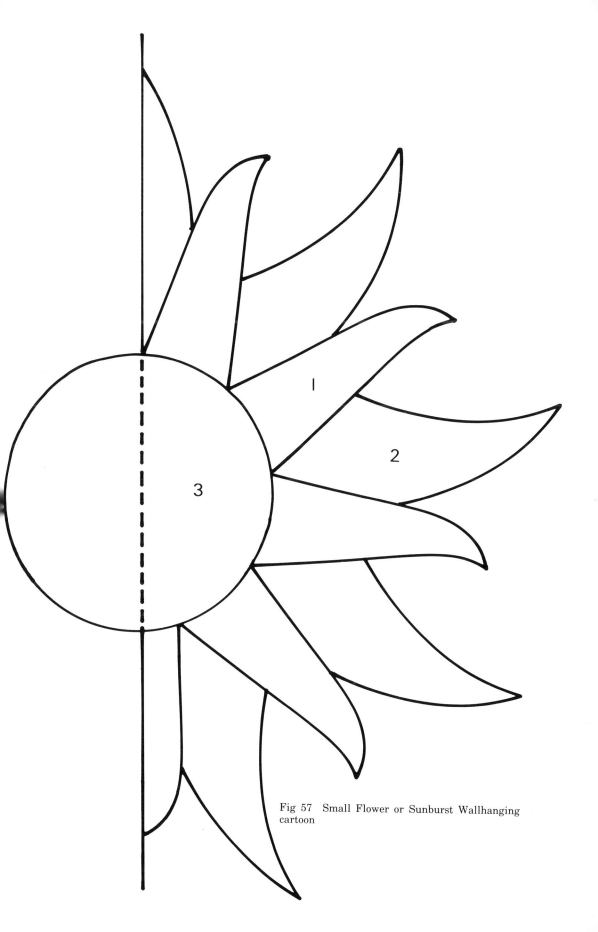

Fig 57   Small Flower or Sunburst Wallhanging cartoon

## Small Flower or Sunburst Wallhanging with Mirror Centre

*Project complexity: 4*
*Assembly technique: foil and lead*
*Composed of 19 pieces of glass*
*Full size cartoon (or enlarge)*

The colour of the glass will determine whether this looks like a flower or a sunburst. For a flower, make the petals (pattern piece 1) pastel opalescent and the leaves (pattern piece 2) an opalescent green. For a sunburst, use yellow opalescent for pattern 1 and orange opalescent for pattern 2. The materials below will make a wallhanging of 9in (22cm) diameter.

*Glass* (for the flower)
3 x 3in (7.5 x 7.5cm) mirror
3 x 10in (7.5 x 25cm) yellow, blue, or violet pastel opalescent
4 x 10in (10 x 25cm) green opalescent
*Glass* (for the sunburst)
3 x 3in (7.5 x 7.5cm) mirror
3 x 10in (7.5 x 25cm) yellow opalescent
4 x 10in (10 x 25cm) orange opalescent

60/40 solder and flux
Copper foil ($\frac{1}{4}$in)
10in (25cm) H-channel lead came ($\frac{1}{4}$in or less)

1 Make a carbon copy of the three pattern pieces on thin poster paper. Cut the pattern apart, removing the line surrounding each piece.
2 Lay each piece on stained glass and draw round it with a glass-marking pen. Cut nine pieces from pattern 1 and nine pieces from pattern 2. Place came around the mirror and wrap copper foil around each of the remaining pieces of glass.
3 Lay all the foiled glass in position around the circular mirror and solder them together. Finish the item by putting a bead of solder along each seam, and add a finishing patina if desired. Do not allow flux or patina to touch the silvered side of the mirror.

A

B

Fig 57a  The petals can all be made to point the same way, as in design B. For this, turn pattern piece 2 over before drawing around it on the glass

## Mirror Edged with Flower Petals

*Project complexity: 4*
*Assembly technique: lead preferred but*
*may be foiled*
*Composed of 46 pieces of glass*
*Cartoon reduced in size (overleaf)*

You can make this flower any size from 18 to 36in (45 to 90cm) in diameter. The smaller size is more of an art object than a functional mirror, whereas the larger size has a 16in (40cm) diameter mirror in the centre. The stem and leaves are optional. The materials below will make a sunflower of 18in (45cm) diameter.

*Glass*
8in (20cm) diameter mirror
Mirror rim: $\frac{1}{4}$sq ft (0.025sq m) amber or white opalescent
Petals: 2sq ft (0.2sq m) yellow or orange opalescent
Leaves and stem: 1sq ft (0.1sq m) green opalescent (stem may be brown)
$\frac{1}{2}$sq ft (0.05sq m) clear glass

60/40 solder and flux
Copper foil ($\frac{1}{4}$in) or H-channel lead came ($\frac{1}{4}$in)

Mirror Edged with Flower Petals

1 Enlarge the cartoon using the grid method described in Chapter 4.
2 On poster paper make a carbon copy of your enlarged cartoon. Number each pattern piece and cut them out, removing the lines around each one.
3 Lay them on stained glass, draw around each piece with a glass-marking pen, and cut the glass just inside the line.
4 Place lead around the mirror and foil or lead the remaining glass as it is cut. Position it over the cartoon and secure with strategically placed nails.
5 The spaces between the leaves and stem are filled with clear glass to give support, though this is unnecessary if the flower measures less than 12in (30cm) across from edge to edge.
6 Tack solder as work progresses. If foil is used instead of lead, place a bead of solder along all seams when all the glass is in position.

Fig 58   Cartoon. Fill shaded areas with clear glass

## Crested-bird Mirror

*Project complexity: 8*
*Assembly technique: H-channel lead*
*Composed of 57 pieces of glass*
*Cartoon reduced in size*

My original of this pair of birds is made of mirror with only the eyes in opalescent glass, but it would also be lovely made completely of opalescent glass. The materials below will make a crested-bird mirror the size of the original, 48in (122cm) long.

9sq ft (1sq m) mirror or opalescent glass
60/40 solder and flux
52ft (16m) H-channel lead came (¼in)
Brass support strap approx ¾in (20mm) wide x ¹⁄₃₂in (0.7mm) thick x 2ft (60cm) long
Brass support strap approx ¾in (20mm) wide x ¹⁄₃₂in (0.7mm) thick x 1½ft (45cm) long

Here are some tips on working with mirror glass. Cut it from the reflecting (not the silvered) side. Do not grind the edges unless you have a wheel that will not chip away the silvered back. If it does become chipped, the reflective quality of

110

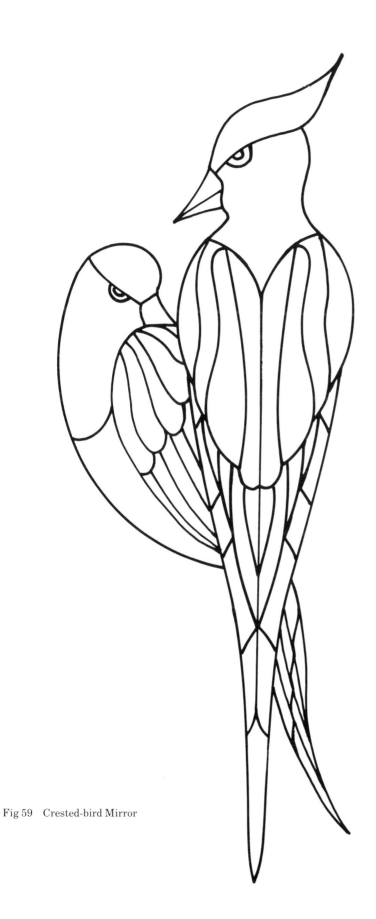

Fig 59   Crested-bird Mirror

the glass is noticeably lost. Be very careful to keep flux and other chemicals (putty or patina) off the back because they will cause the silvered surface to deteriorate.

1 The original mirrored birds measure 48in (122cm) long x 21in (53cm) wide, but they can be made much smaller and still retain their elegance. Enlarge the cartoon to your chosen size using the grid method described in Chapter 4.

2 On light poster paper make a carbon copy of the enlarged cartoon. Number each pattern piece and the cartoon with corresponding numbers. Cut the pieces apart and remove the line between them.

3 Place each pattern piece on mirror, draw around it with a glass-marking pen, and cut just inside the pattern line. Lay the glass over the cartoon and fit lead came around the glass. Solder the came together after several pieces are in position. When the front is completely soldered together, turn the birds over using two boards. Sandwich the birds firmly between the two boards and then quickly turn them over (this will require a helper). Solder the back, being careful not to get flux on the silvered backing of the mirror.

4 Push putty under the came on the *front* of the panel but not the back. Do not thin the putty; leave it thick and viscous so that it does not ooze through to the silvered side. Clean as usual with sawdust.

5 Support straps are needed with this design if the panel is 30in (76cm) or more long. They must be flat metal strips, as the birds will be displayed flush against a wall. Solder one or two brass or copper strips to the lead on the silvered back. Again, avoid getting flux on the silvered surface.

6 Hang the mirror on five nails positioned as shown in the wall to correspond to the sweep of the design. Hold the birds against the wall to mark the nail positions.

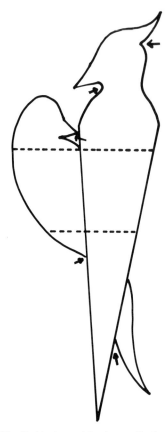

Fig 60   Guide to positioning nails (arrowed) and support rods (dotted lines) for hanging Crested-bird Mirror

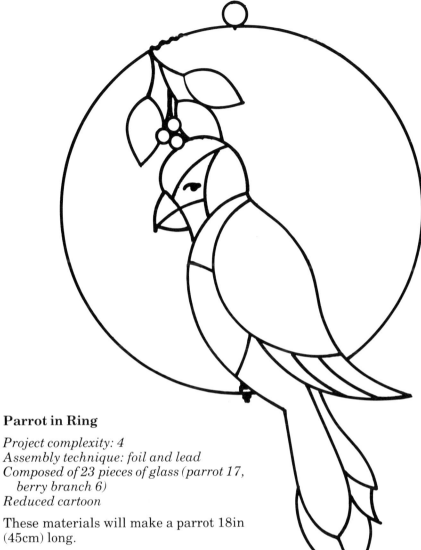

## Parrot in Ring

*Project complexity: 4*
*Assembly technique: foil and lead*
*Composed of 23 pieces of glass (parrot 17,*
*   berry branch 6)*
*Reduced cartoon*

These materials will make a parrot 18in
(45cm) long.

Scrap glass in a variety of colours
3 red glass nuggets (¹/₂in or ³/₄in)
60/40 solder and flux
Copper foil (¹/₄in)
6ft (2m) U-channel lead (¹/₈in)
Ring, preferably wooden, 12-14in (30-35cm)
   diameter
15in (38cm) firm wire
Nut and bolt, 1¹/₂in (38mm) long

Fig 61   Parrot in Ring, showing complete design.
Cartoon overleaf (colour photograph page 35)

1 Enlarge the design using the grid
method in Chapter 4. Make a copy of the
enlarged cartoon and number each piece.
Cut one copy apart to be used as the
pattern.

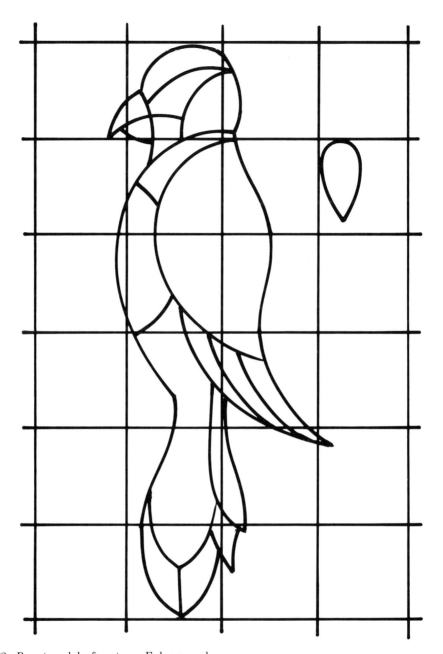

Fig 62 Parrot and leaf cartoon. Enlarge each
square to 3in (75mm) to make a parrot 18in (45cm)
long. Cut three leaves

2 Lay each pattern piece on glass, draw around it with a glass-marking pen and cut the glass.

3 Place foil around the glass, lay it in position over the cartoon, tape the pieces together and then solder them. Place a solder bead over all the solder lines on both sides.

4 Paint in the parrot's eye.

5 Place U-channel lead around the parrot and solder the lead where it intersects a foiled line.

6 Drill a hole in the wooden (or plastic) ring to accommodate the long bolt. Drill another hole directly opposite the first for a hanging bolt or screw eye, and drill a third hole for the wire 'stem' of the berry branch. This should be 3-4in (7.5-10cm) from the second hole (see Fig 63).

7 Hold the parrot in the ring and determine the angle it should sit. Mark the lead where it rests on the ring, and solder the bolt to the parrot at that point. The head of the bolt will not be flat against the lead came, but rather at an angle—fill the gap created with solder (see Fig 63). Make certain that solder flows completely over the head of the bolt. Place the bolt through the hole in the ring, screw on the nut, cut off the excess bolt shaft with bolt cutters, and solder the nut to the bolt.

8 Next, prepare the cluster of berries, which adds support to the precariously perched parrot. Wrap the nuggets and leaves in foil and cover the foil with solder. Lay the leaves and berries in a pleasing pattern and solder them together with pieces of wire. The wire 'stem' must be long enough to extend through the hole in the ring and wrap around it once or twice.

9 Position the berry branch so it touches the head of the parrot and solder.

10 Place a hanging loop into the hole at the top of the ring and add a chain or cord of the desired length.

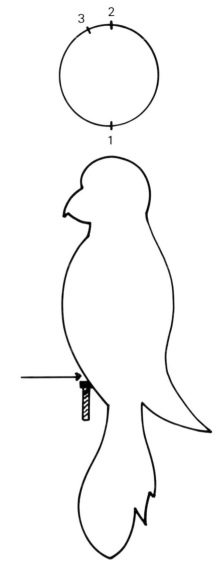

Fig 63   Make three holes in the ring as shown: the bolt goes through hole 1; the hanging loop through 2; and the wire with leaves through 3. Fill the arrowed area with solder

Fig 64   Unicorn (colour photograph page 36)

116

## Unicorn

*Project complexity: 5*
*Assembly technique: lead preferred but it*
*    may be foiled*
*Composed of 36 pieces of glass*
*Reduced cartoon. Enlarge as described in*
*    Chapter 4*

The mythical unicorn has charmed mankind since the Greeks created it. This one is an innocent young creature bedecked with jewels and surrounded by greenery. If the panel is to be used as a wallhanging, make the background of mirror; but if it is to be hung in a window, use clear seedy for background; or, if you prefer, the background could be left open. The 'jewels' around the horn can be either faceted glass jewels or ¾in (20mm) glass nuggets which are much less expensive. The items listed will make a 16 x 30in (40 x 76cm) unicorn.

*Glass*
Leaves: 1⅓sq ft (0.12sq m) green opalescent
Head, neck and ears: 1½sq ft (0.14sq m) dark
    amber or caramel
Mane: 1sq ft (0.1sq m) light-amber opalescent
Base of horn: 5 nuggets or jewels (¾in or
    20mm)

60/40 solder and flux
20ft (7m) H-channel lead (¼in) *or* copper foil
    (¼in)

## Old English Alphabet

These letters are an adaptation of the Old English alphabet. Some are quite complicated and composed of many pattern pieces, but these patterns can be altered to fit your needs. Include all the pieces if large letters are to be made, but eliminate some of the smaller pieces in smaller letters. They can be used singly as an initial, combined into a name or title, or incorporated into a composition. A letter that is not surrounded by glass is, of course, much easier to make. Otherwise, make graceful lines in the background glass to facilitate the glass cutting.

Fig 65   Old English Alphabet

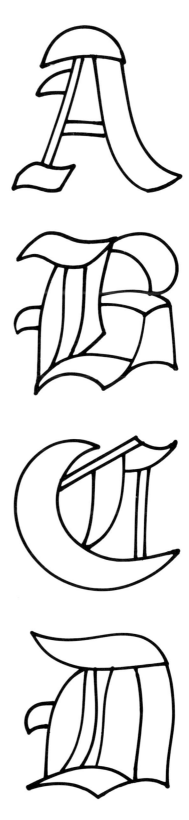

117

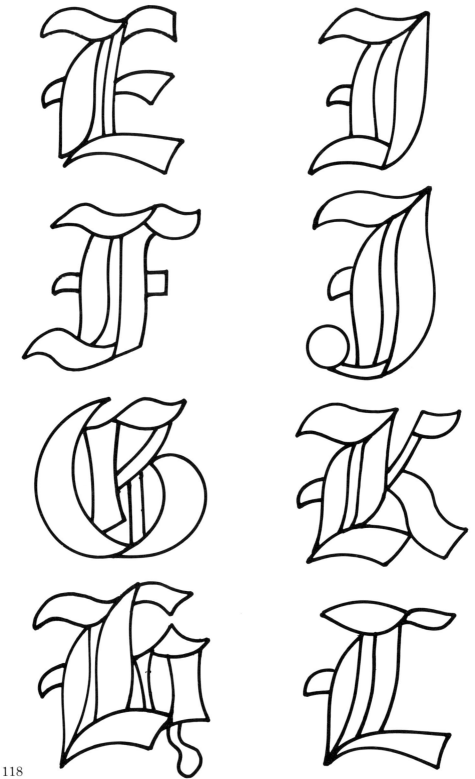

119

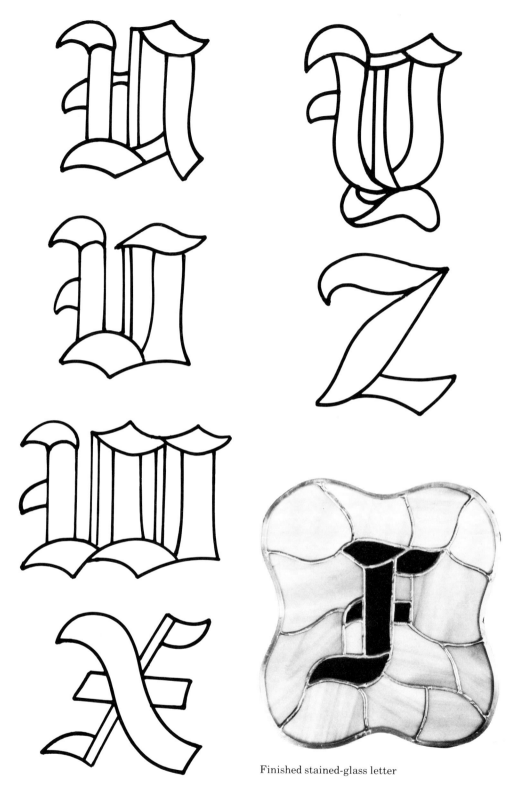

Finished stained-glass letter

## Miniature House Night Light

*Project complexity: 6*
*Assembly technique: foil*
*Composed of 55 pieces of glass*
*Full-sized cartoon*

*Glass*
Front, back and sides: 8 x 8in (20 x 20cm) any
colour opalescent
Windows and door: 2 x 4in (5 x 10cm) opalescent yellow, dark purple and black
Roof and porch roof: 6 x 6in (15 x 15cm) opalescent tile red
Porch floor: 2 x 5in (5 x 13cm) opalescent light
amber

60/40 solder and flux
Copper foil (¼in)

1 Make two carbon copies of the house
front cartoon, cutting on the solid lines.
Cut one copy apart by putting away the
pencil line between the pieces. Construct
the panels of the house over the other copy
of the cartoon. For the back, either repeat
the front or cut one plain piece of glass.
2 Cut and foil the pieces of glass. Cut narrow slivers of foil and place these on the
windows and the door to represent window bars and for decoration. Place the
pieces over the cartoon, make certain the
sides are square, and solder them together. Cover the window bars etc with
solder. Turn over and solder the seams on
the other side.
3 Make up two side panels in the same
way. After all four sides have been completed, stand them together and fill in the
corners with solder as shown in Fig f.
4 Each roof panel overhangs a side and
both ends of the house. Solder the roof to
the top of the gables and fill in the roof
ridge with solder.
5 Solder the porch-roof pieces together,
with 90° angles at corners to produce a
sloping roof as shown in Fig g. There are
three horizontal lines around the walls of
the house. The middle line indicates the
floor level of the upstairs rooms and the
porch roof is attached to this line. Solder
along the top of the porch roof, filling the
space with solder.

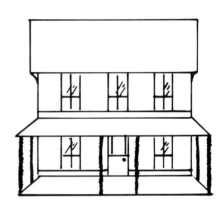

Fig a    Views of Miniature House Night Light

6 Solder the porch-floor pieces together,
set the house inside the porch floor, making the two floors level. Solder together
the bottom edge of the house and the inside edge of the porch floor.
7 The porch pillars and gable trim are
made by twisting together two strands of
wire. Cut the eight pillars to fit between
the porch floor and roof. Position them as
shown on the cartoon and solder. Add
wire trim to the gables for added support
(see Fig h).
8 Use a 7 watt Christmas-tree or night-
light bulb to light this miniature house.

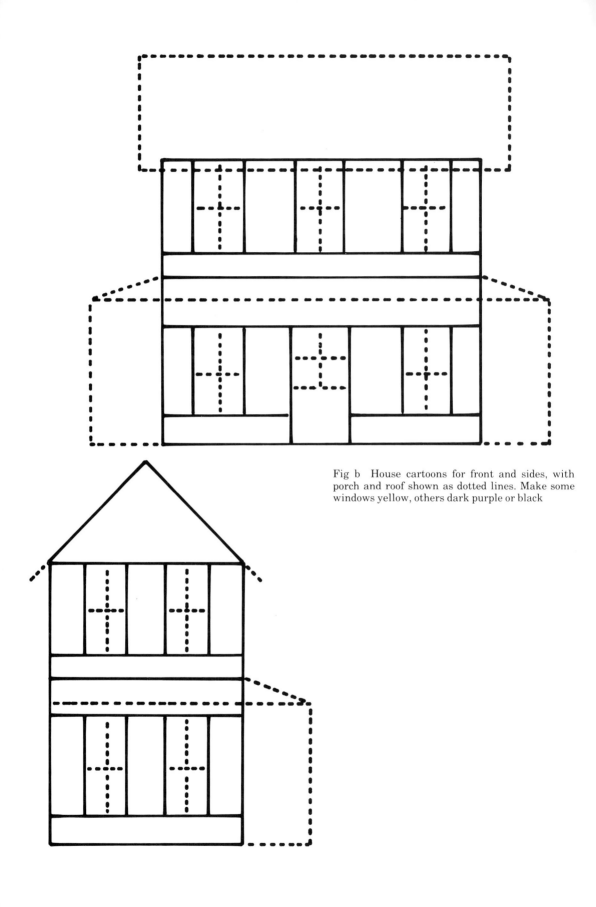

Fig b  House cartoons for front and sides, with porch and roof shown as dotted lines. Make some windows yellow, others dark purple or black

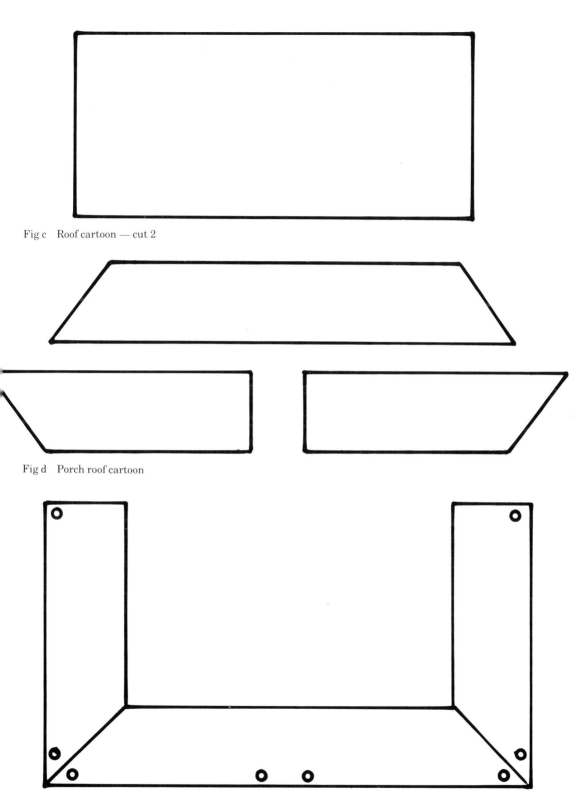

Fig c    Roof cartoon — cut 2

Fig d    Porch roof cartoon

Fig e    Porch floor cartoon. Circles indicate positions of pillars

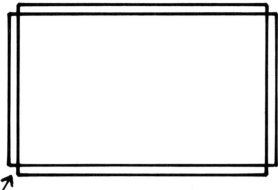

Fig f  View from above of house walls joined together. Fill corners with solder as arrowed

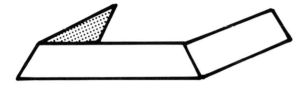

Fig g  Solder together the porch roof, with 90°
angles at corners

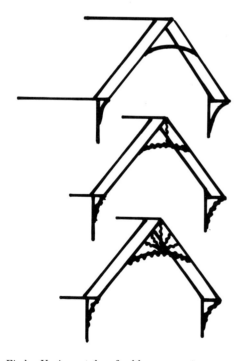

Fig h  Various styles of gable ornament

COLOUR PLATE
Life in Space (page 162)

# 7  Lamp Shades

Stained glass is a natural for lamp shades. They are usually made with opalescent glass because it transmits an even glow, while hiding the fitting and bulb. Tiffany-style lamps with intricate designs are foiled, but straight-edged lamps can be either foiled or leaded. Dome-shaped shades with curved sides are made on forms available from stained-glass suppliers (see Suppliers). The form may be a complete circular shape, but most are a ⅙th section of the lamp shade. Six identical sections are made over the form and then soldered edge to edge into a unit. The forms determine the shape and maintain it during construction. They come in a wide variety of shapes and sizes. Panel shades, with flat sides, are constructed in sections over a cartoon on a building board and then soldered together into a 'circular' shade.

Cartoons and instructions for foiled dome and panel shades are given in this chapter, but you might also like to design and build a leaded panel shade. This is quite simple but there are several factors to keep in mind. Leaded panel shades must have a minimum of eight straight-edged panels (see Fig 67). With fewer panels, the angles between them will be too great, sometimes forcing the lead to be bent so much that the edges of the glass might slip from the came overlap. When leading a lamp, use H-channel lead between the panels, and U-channel lead along the bottom and top edges for a finished appearance (leave off the came around the top until after the shade has been bent into shape). Place a minimum of solder on the inside joints of the shade,

COLOUR PLATE
May Bouquet (page 163)

then carefully pick up the tack-soldered panels and bend each joint until the two ends meet. Tape the two ends together and solder. Proceed to solder all of the lead joints on the outside of the shade, then add more solder to the tack-soldered joints on the inside of the shade. Finally, place U-channel came around the top edge and solder.

## Designing Panel Lamp Shades

1 Draw a triangle whose shape is of the same proportion as the desired shade in profile. The slope of the shade will be determined by the height of the triangle. The base of the triangle represents the base of the shade and its diameter. The height of the shade is established by drawing a line parallel to the bottom line as shown in Fig 68A. This truncated triangle is the lamp shade in profile.
2 Next, determine the circumference of the shade by multiplying the base diameter by 3.14 (pi).
3 Select the number of panels to be in the shade and divide the circumference by that number to determine the width of each panel at its base.
4 Draw an arc whose radius is the length of the triangle side, from the base to the vertex. Draw a second arc to represent the top opening of the shade, see Fig 68B.
5 Starting at any point on the outer arc, measure and mark the width of each panel base as determined by 3 above. Draw lines from the marks on the outer arc to the vertex to define the shape of the panels.
6 Before cutting the panels from glass, cut full-size pattern pieces from cardboard and tape them together to evaluate the shape of the shade, and the accuracy with which the several panels will join together.

127

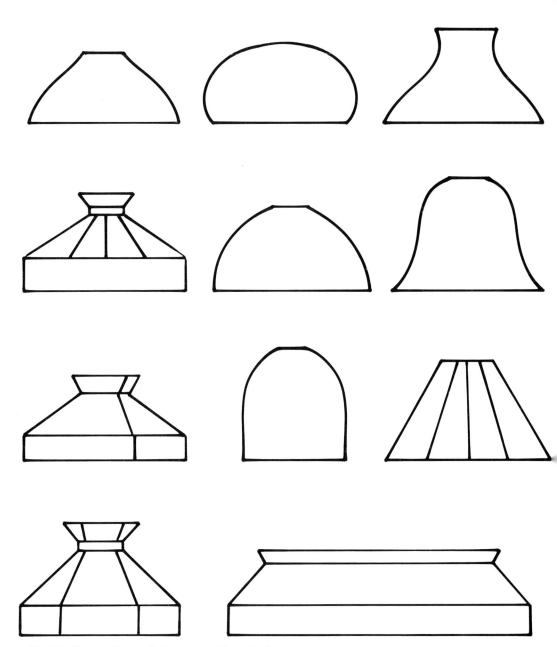

Fig 66    Shapes of lamp shades made with stained
glass

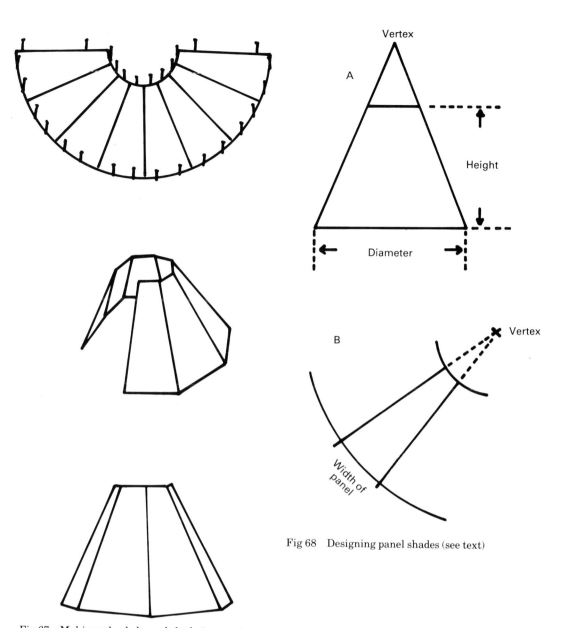

Vertex

A

Height

Diameter

B

Width of panel

Vertex

Fig 68   Designing panel shades (see text)

Fig 67   Making a leaded panel shade (see text)

## Shasta Daisy Lamp

*Project complexity: 8*
*Assembly technique: foil*
*Composed of 60 or 348 pieces of glass (see below)*
*Base diameter: 20in (51cm)*
*Full size cartoon*

This lamp is made on a 20in (51cm) cone, sectional moulded form, known as a Tiffany Kit in the UK (see Suppliers). The lamp can be made three different ways (detailed instructions are given for Plan 1, the most difficult).

Plan 1: This plan will produce a lamp shade made of 348 pieces of glass. Each leaf is composed of twelve pieces of glass.

Plan 2: Use only the centre and petal pieces numbered 1, 2, 3, and 4. This shade is slightly smaller than Plan 1 but is much easier to construct. It is crafted of 60 pieces of glass and has no leaves.

Plan 3: Use only the centre and petal pieces numbered 1, 2, 3, and 4, but make the small edge petals (4) green, thereby converting them into leaves. This shade is also composed of 60 pieces of glass.

*Glass for Plan 1*
Centre (piece no 1): ½sq ft (0.05sq m) brown or yellow opalescent
Petals (piece nos 2, 3, 4): 3½sq ft (0.33sq m) pastel opalescent
Leaves (piece no 5): 2sq ft (0.2sq m) green opalescent

*Glass for Plan 2*
Centre (piece no 1): ½sq ft (0.05sq m) brown or yellow opalescent
Petals (piece nos 2, 3, 4): 3½sq ft (0.33 sq m) pastel opalescent

*Glass for Plan 3*
Centre (piece no 1): ½sq ft (0.05sq m) brown or yellow opalescent
Petals (piece nos 2, 3): 3sq ft (0.3sq m) pastel opalescent
Leaves (piece no 4): 1 sq ft (0.1sq m) green opalescent

60/40 solder and flux
Copper foil (7/32in or ¼in)

1 This lamp shade (Plan 1) is made in six sections, each consisting of the pieces shown in Fig 70.

2 On sturdy poster paper, make a carbon copy of the pattern pieces and cut them apart by cutting away the pen or pencil line.

3 Place each pattern piece on glass, draw around it with a glass-marking pen and cut just inside the line. Cut only six of the required twelve pieces of glass from pattern no 2. Wrap each piece in foil and carefully smooth the edges to eliminate wrinkles and to assure good adhesion. Place the foiled pieces of one section in position on the styrofoam lamp form and hold them in place with straight pins. When all pieces of the section are in place, tack solder all joints with the least amount of heat possible. Remove the glass from the lamp form, turn the section over and solder the back completely with the front on a wet towel to absorb the heat. Then, with the back on a wet towel, complete the soldering on the front. Place a bead of solder along each of the seams. This is a time consuming task requiring a large amount of solder, but it is necessary for the finish and to strengthen the shade.

4 After all six sections have been completed, solder them together. Some will fit together better than others so try various arrangements until you find the best sequence.

5 Using pattern piece no 2 cut glass to fill the holes between the sections. Check the size of the pattern for each opening and alter if necessary. When the pattern piece fits the opening, draw it on glass, cut and foil the glass, and solder it into place.

6 Solder a cap to the opening at the top of the lamp and wire the lamp as shown in Fig 72.

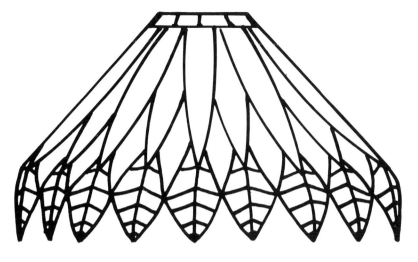

Plan 1

Plan 2

Plan 3

Fig 69   Shasta Daisy Lamp, the three plans (colour photographs page 53)

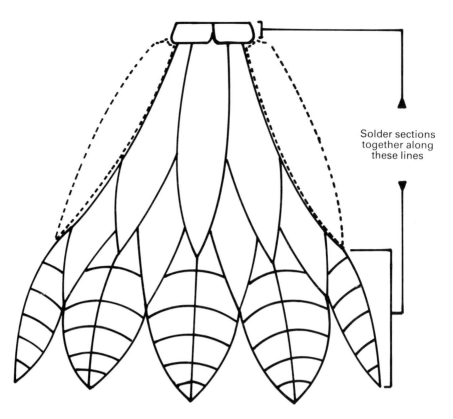

Solder sections
together along
these lines

Fig 70 The lamp is made in six sections like the
one shown here. After all of the sections are completed, solder them together, and fill the holes between the sections with petals cut from pattern piece
2 (dashed lines). Before cutting the petals to fill the
openings, check pattern size

*Opposite*
Fig 71 Pattern for Shasta Daisy Lamp
1 Cut twelve, two per section
2 Cut twelve, one per section, plus six used to fill
openings between sections (see Fig 70). Cut these
six *after* the sections have been made, to check fit
3 Cut twelve, two per section
4 Cut twenty-four, four per section
5 Cut twenty-four of each separate piece within 5.
Each section has three full leaves and two half
leaves (see Fig 70)

132

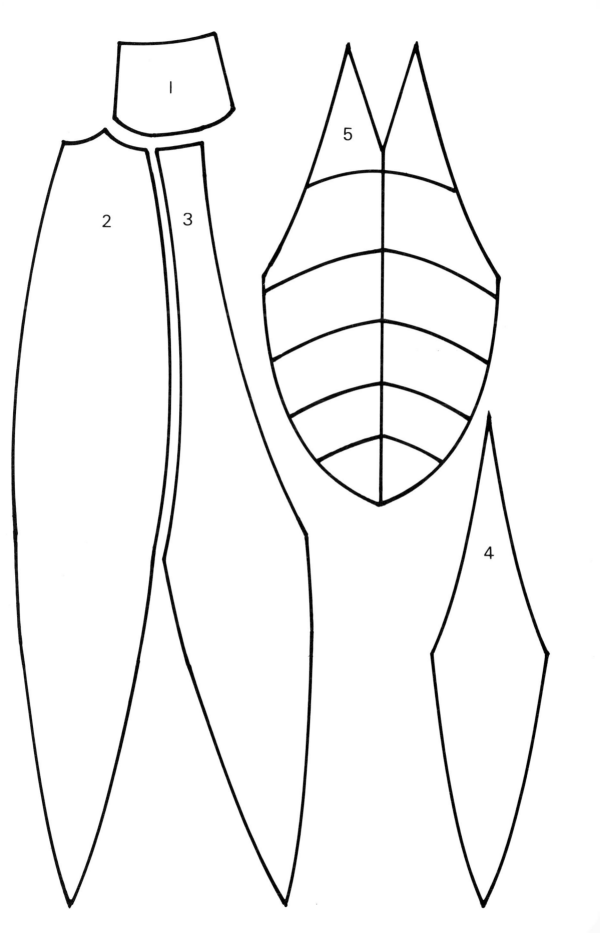

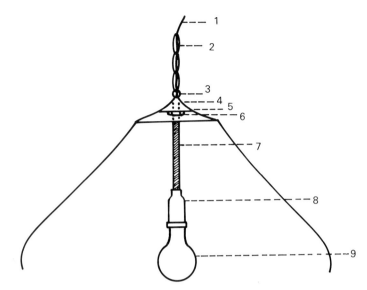

Fig 72   Wiring lamp

1  Wire cord
2  Chain
3  Loop ring
4  Vase cap
5  Washer
6  Locknut
7  Threaded tubing
8  Socket
9  Bulb (use globe bulb if available)

*Instructions for wiring lamp*
Remove about 1in (25mm) of the plastic or rubber insulation from the ends of the lamp cord and fit a wall plug on one end. Thread the other end through the components on the lamp, from the chain to the socket, and attach the bared ends of the wire to the screws in the socket. This is the most direct and simple way to wire a lamp. If you wish to add more elaborate fixtures, consult your local lamp or electrical shop for advice.

**Flower Panel Lamp**

*Project complexity: 9*
*Assembly technique: foil*
*Composed of 318 pieces of glass*
*Top diameter: 9in (23cm); bottom diameter: 22in (55cm)*
*Full size cartoon*

This is a three-section geometric lamp with six panels in each section (see Fig 73). The panels within each section are constructed over a cartoon on a flat surface and then soldered together.

*Glass*
Background: 5sq ft (0.5sq m)
Leaves: 4sq ft (0.4sq m)
Flowers: 1½sq ft (0.14sq m)
Jewels or nuggets: six 1in (25mm); six ¾in (20mm)

60/40 solder and flux
Copper foil (¼in)

1 Make two copies of the cartoon in this book. Cut one apart to use as the pattern, and cut away the pencil line around each pattern piece.
2 Cut, foil, and solder the glass pieces for each panel. Solder the foil seams of each panel, back and front.
3 When the six panels of section B are

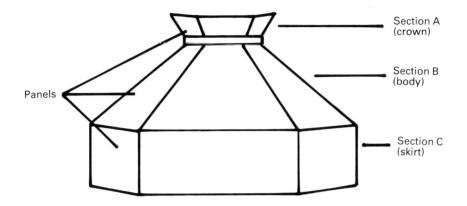

Fig 73 Components of a panel lamp (colour photograph page 54)

complete, solder them together. To do this, stand the panels up in a circle on the work table. With the lower edge of the panels on the table, bring the side edges together to form an open-ended cone. Use masking tape to hold the pieces in position and tack solder (see Fig 74). Place a damp cloth against the back of each seam and solder the seams completely. Then solder the inside seams.

4 To section B, add the panels of the skirt, one at a time, and tack solder in position. When all are in place, solder the seams completely, again using a damp cloth against the back of the seam. Add the crown next. The crown can be attached directly to the body, *or* a strip of brass can be inserted between the crown and the body of the shade to support the lamp.

5 Cut two brass strips, each 1in (25mm) wide, to reach across the top of section B. Drill a ³⁄₈in (10mm) hole in the centre of the strips and solder them to the inside of the top of section B, forming a cross as shown in Fig 74.

6 Wire the lamp as described in the previous lamp project.

**Versatile Six-panel Shade Design**

This basic design will yield a lamp shade with a bottom width of 12in (30cm) and a top opening of 4in (10cm). Each panel can be a single piece of glass, or it can be divided into a design. Sample designs are provided (see Fig 81). The shade is composed of only six panels, so it should be foiled.

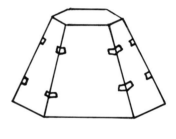

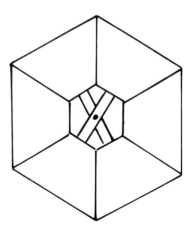

Fig 74 Assembling the Flower Panel Lamp

135

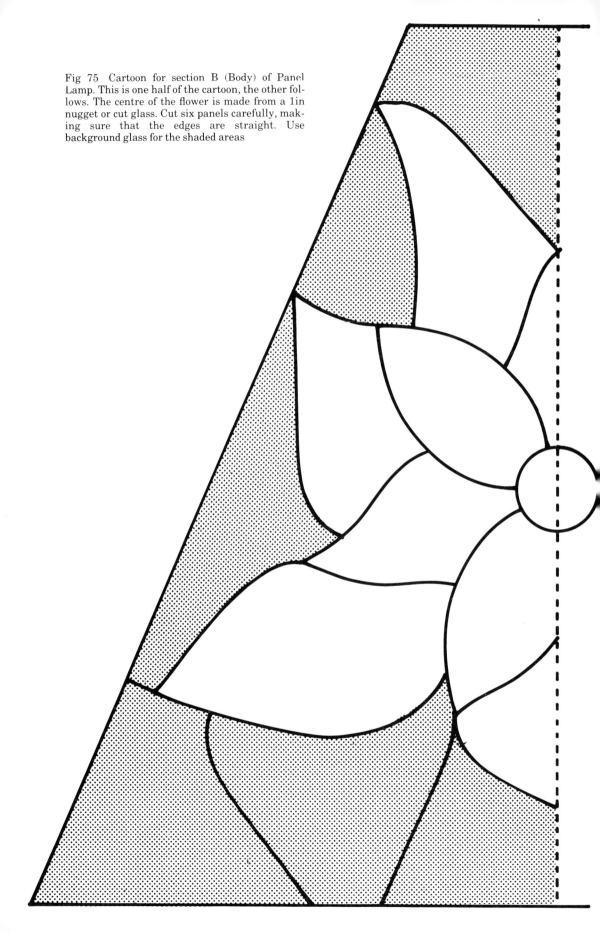

Fig 75 Cartoon for section B (Body) of Panel Lamp. This is one half of the cartoon, the other follows. The centre of the flower is made from a 1in nugget or cut glass. Cut six panels carefully, making sure that the edges are straight. Use background glass for the shaded areas

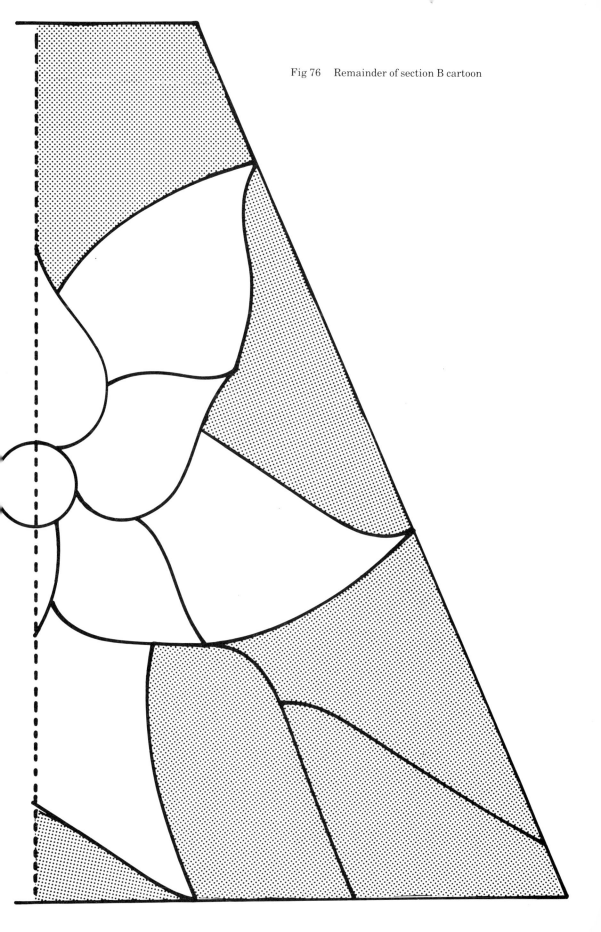

Fig 76    Remainder of section B cartoon

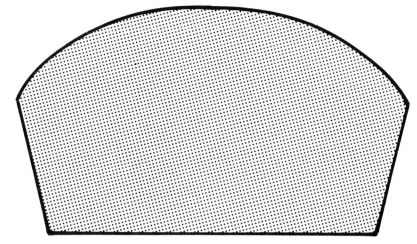

Fig 77  Cartoon for section A (crown). Cut six

Fig 78  Cartoon for section C (Skirt). This is one half of the cartoon, the other follows. The flower centre is a ³⁄₄in nugget, or cut glass. Cut six panels

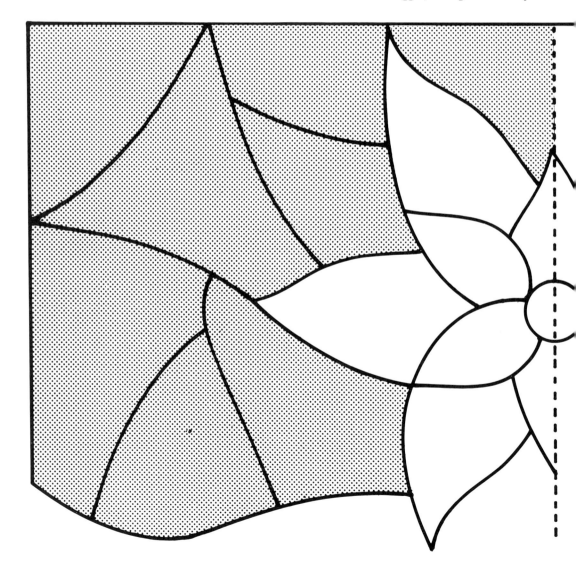

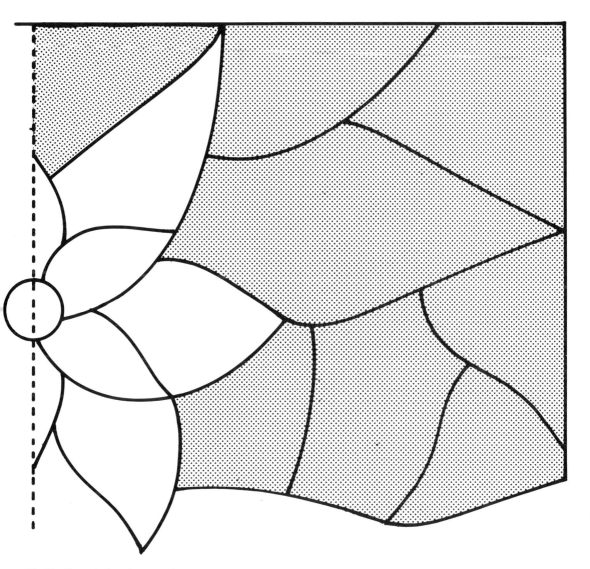

Fig 79    Remainder of section C cartoon

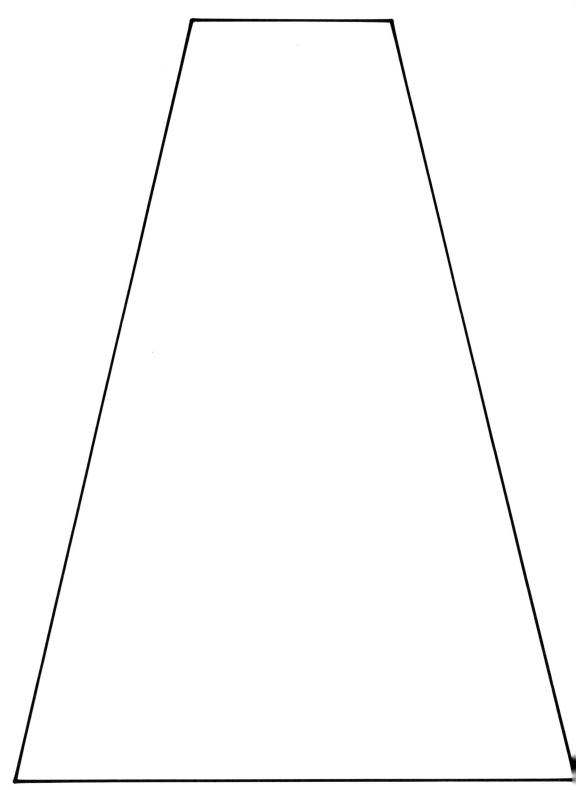

Fig 80  Cartoon for Six-panel Shade. Cut six
panels

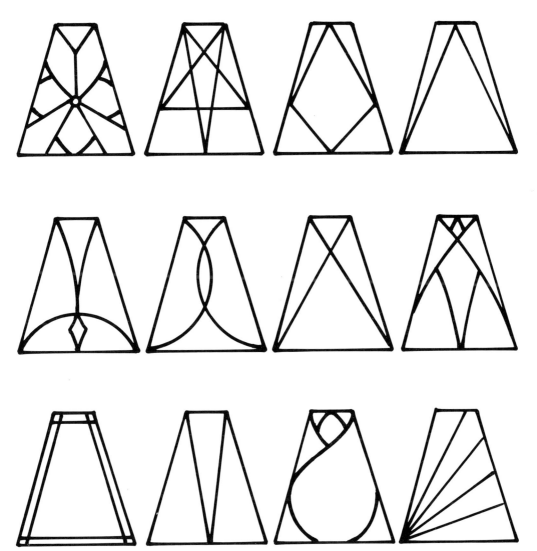

Fig 81 Ideas for designs to use for the Six-panel Shade

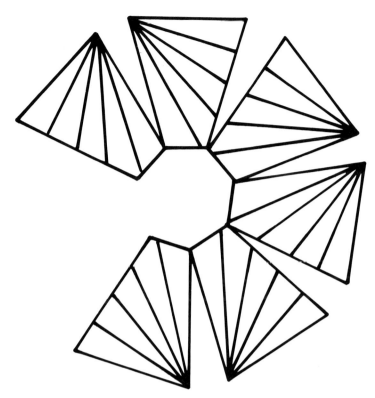

Fig 82   If the final design in Fig 81 is used, the panels can be combined to create this pattern

COLOUR PLATE
Energy (page 164)
Peeper (page 166)

# 8  Window Patterns

Stained-glass windows are a delight, introducing coloured light that dances and plays within your home, and changing throughout the day with the different angles and intensities of the sun's rays.

The following window cartoons include a variety of styles. They can be enlarged to fill your needs by using the grid method described in Chapter 4. If a pattern is not the right proportions for a given area, alter it by eliminating edges or by extending the lines. This procedure will work for most of the patterns that follow. These windows can either be foiled or leaded, although they will be stronger and neater if they are leaded. It is wise to use a zinc border for added support on large windows. Use a border of ½in wide zinc for windows of 4sq ft (0.4sq m) or more.

Plan a project carefully before beginning, as, once a panel is completed, it is difficult to alter. Give the project time to evolve so that it becomes an interesting and unusual composition rather than something copied verbatim from a book. You might use the cartoons in this book as a guide, altering them to your ideas, but, if you are not inclined to try your hand at design, then spend your energy selecting the perfect glass with which to construct the panels. In this way, you can put your personal touch on every stained-glass item you make.

### Peace

*Project complexity: 8*
*Composed of 167 pieces of glass*

The materials given will make a panel 16 x 60in (40 x 152cm).

COLOUR PLATE
Where in the Hell is the Yellow Ribbon? (page 166)

Fig 83   Peace (colour photograph page 71)

*Glass*
Background: 4sq ft (0.4sq m) amber
Leaves: ½sq ft (0.05sq m) green
Columns: 3sq ft (0.3sq m) violet
Trim on top: ½sq ft (0.05sq m) red
Circle and arch: 1¼sq ft (0.12sq m) aqua
Flower: ⅛sq ft (0.012sq m) white
12 jewels or ¼sq ft (0.025sq m) yellow glass
Top and bottom column: 1½sq ft (0.14sq m)
  light green
Circle rim: ⅓sq ft (0.03sq m) amber
  cathedral

60/40 solder and flux
74ft (22.5m) H-channel lead (¼in)
13ft (4m) zinc (½in)

## Miss Universe

*Project complexity: 8*
*Composed of 124 pieces of glass*

This panel was designed to be used in a corner against the ceiling and adjacent walls, with a fluorescent tube at the intersection of the walls. The materials given will make a triangular panel measuring 36in (1m) on each edge.

*Glass*
Skin: 3sq ft (0.3sq m) amber opalescent
Hair: 1sq ft (0.1sq m) different purples
Border: 1½sq ft (0.14sq m) your choice
Background: 3sq ft (0.3sq m) dark blue
  opalescent
Star: ½sq ft (0.05sq m) white opalescent
Sun and moon: 1sq ft (0.1sq m) yellow
  opalescent
Small pieces of red and black

60/40 solder and flux
96ft (32m) H-channel lead (¼in)
10ft (3.5m) zinc (½in wide)

Miss Universe panel

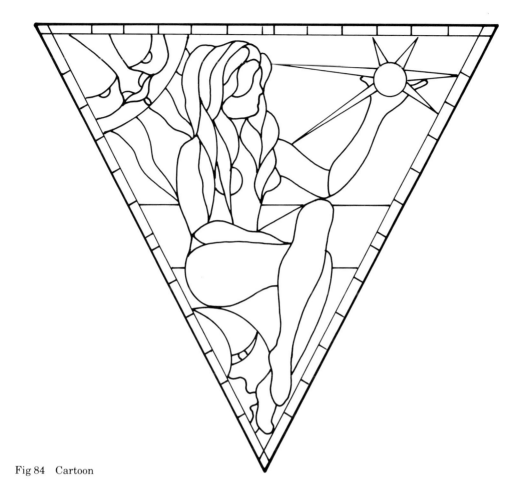

Fig 84   Cartoon

## Skyline 1 and Skyline 2

*Project complexity: 5*
*Composed of 107(1) or 123(2) pieces of*
*  glass*

The material given will make a panel 18
x 24in (45 x 60cm). A glass grinder with a
small head is needed to cut the glass in
Skyline 2. If you do not have a grinder,
use Skyline 1 (cartoons overleaf).

Make the cross bars on the windows
with narrow strips of copper foil. Press
the foil to the glass before placing the
glass in position.

*Glass*
Windows: ⅛sq ft (0.012sq m) black or very
  dark purple cathedral
Houses: 3sq ft (0.3sq m) your choice opalescent
Sun or moon and windows: ½sq ft (0.05sq m)
  yellow opalescent
Sky: 1½sq ft (0.14sq m) dark blue opalescent

60/40 solder and flux
36ft (11m) H-channel lead (¼in)
8ft (2.5m) zinc (½in wide)
Foil (¼in)

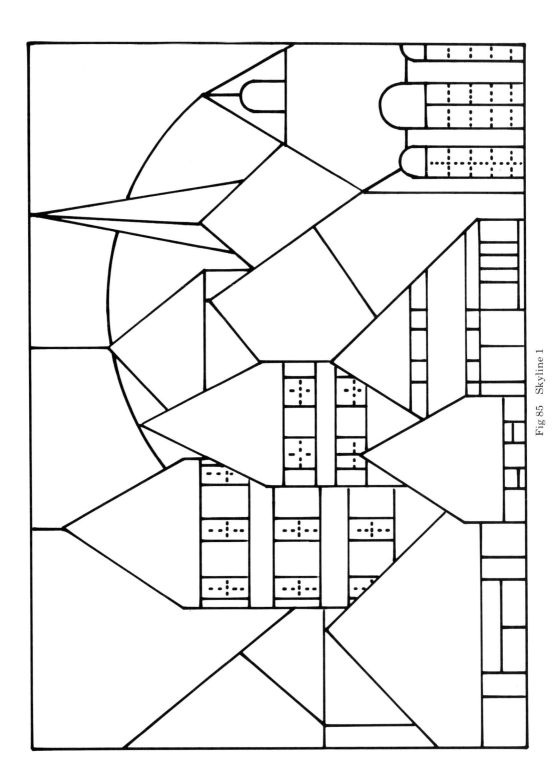

Fig 85  Skyline 1

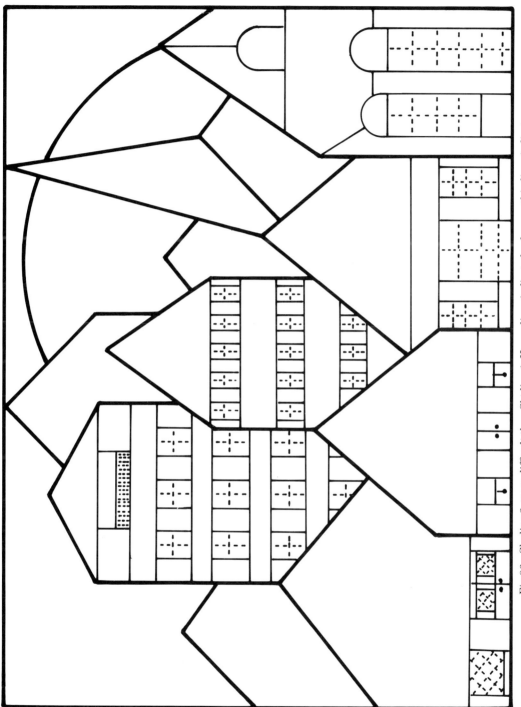

Fig 86  Skyline 2, more difficult than Skyline 1. Heavy lines indicate lead came, thin lines indicate foil, and dashed lines indicate narrow strips of copper overlay (colour photograph page 54)

## Swan with Cygnets

Fig 87   Swan with Cygnets

*Project complexity: 6*
*Composed of 110 pieces of glass*

The materials given will make a panel 24
x 24in (60 x 60cm).

*Glass*
Leaves: 1sq ft (0.1sq m) green opalescent
Swan: 1½sq ft (0.14 sq m) white opalescent
Face: 1 x 2in (25mm x 50mm) red
Cygnets: ⅓sq ft (0.031sq m) yellow opalescent
Sky background: 2½sq ft (0.25sq m) blue
    opalescent
Swan bill and sun: ½sq ft (0.05sq m) orange
    or yellow opalescent

Water: ½sq ft (0.05sq m) blue opalescent
Border: 1sq ft (0.1sq m) your choice
Rushes (cattails): ⅛sq ft (0.012sq m) brown

60/40 solder and flux
40ft (12m) H-channel lead (¼in)
12ft (4m) zinc (½in wide)

150

## Cardinal in Summer

*Project complexity: 5*
*Composed of 83 pieces of glass*

The materials given will make a panel measuring 11 x 25in (28 x 63.5cm).

*Glass*
Bird: $\frac{1}{8}$sq ft (0.012sq m) red cathedral
Tree: $\frac{1}{3}$sq ft (0.031sq m) brown opalescent
Leaves: $\frac{3}{4}$sq ft (0.07sq m) green opalescent
Sky: $\frac{1}{2}$sq ft (0.05sq m) blue
Sun: $\frac{1}{2}$sq ft (0.05sq m) yellow
Grass: $\frac{3}{4}$sq ft (0.07sq m) green
Border: $\frac{1}{2}$sq ft (0.05sq m) your choice

60/40 solder and flux
24ft (7.5m) H-channel lead ($\frac{1}{4}$in)

Fig 88   Cardinal in Summer

## Cardinal in Winter

*Project complexity: 5*
*Composed of 65 pieces of glass*

The materials given will make a panel measuring 11 x 25in (28 x 63.5cm).

*Glass*
Bird: $\frac{1}{8}$sq ft (0.012sq m) red cathedral
Sun: $\frac{1}{2}$sq ft (0.05sq m) purple cathedral
Sky: 1sq ft (0.1sq m) pale blue opalescent
Snow: $\frac{3}{4}$sq ft (0.07sq m) white opalescent
Tree: $\frac{1}{3}$sq ft (0.031sq m) brown opalescent
Border: $\frac{1}{2}$sq ft (0.05sq m) your choice

60/40 solder and flux
24ft (7.5m) H-channel lead ($\frac{1}{4}$in)

Fig 89   Cartoon

Cardinal in Winter panel

152

## Duck with Young

*Project complexity: 6*
*Composed of 146 pieces of glass*

The two panels of this project were designed to be used in adjacent windows, but the design can be altered and each half used separately for a single window. The materials given will make both panels, each measuring 12 x 32in (30 x 81.3cm).

*Glass*
Sky: 2sq ft (0.2sq m) blue or clear seedy
Sun: 2sq ft (0.2sq m) yellow opalescent
Baby ducks: ¾sq ft (0.07sq m) brown opalescent
Leaves: 1sq ft (0.1sq m) green opalescent
Rushes (cattails): ¼sq ft (0.025sq m) brown cathedral
Border: 1½sq ft (0.14sq m) your choice
Duck bills: ¹⁄₁₆sq ft (0.006sq m) orange opalescent
Duck: ⅛sq ft (0.012sq m) green cathedral
Duck: ⅛sq ft (0.012sq m) dark purple cathedral
Duck: ⅛sq ft (0.012sq m) blue cathedral
Small pieces of red and white

60/40 solder and flux
56ft (17m) H-channel lead (¼in)
16ft (4.8m) zinc (½in wide)

Fig 90   Duck with Young, designed for the top of a double window (enlarged cartoons overleaf). The dashed lines indicate altered positions for the setting sun if the panels are used separately (do not forget to delete the existing line)

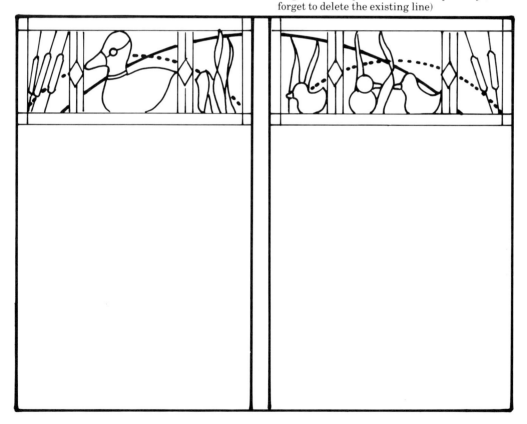

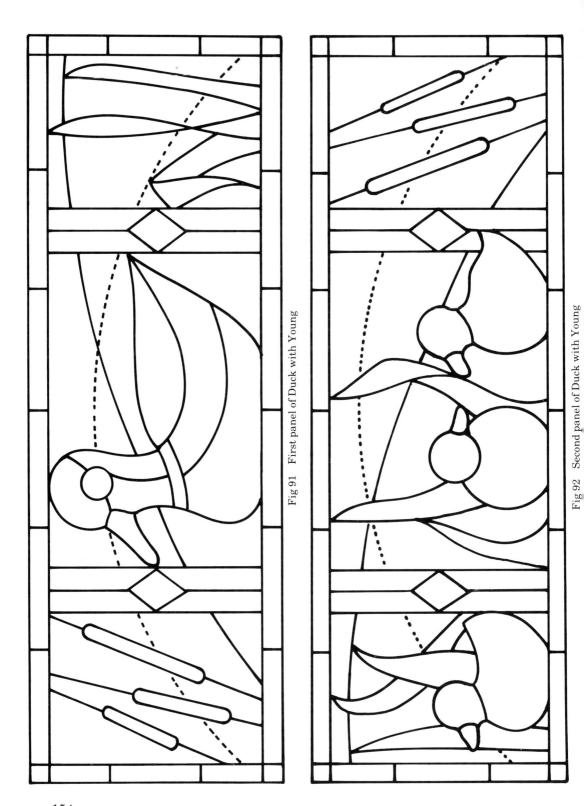

Fig 91   First panel of Duck with Young

Fig 92   Second panel of Duck with Young

Fig 93   Onion

Fig 94   Tulip

155

## Tulip or Onion

*Project complexity: 4*
*Composed of 68 (tulip) or 55 (onion) pieces of glass*

This panel has been designed to be used along the top of a window frame or in a door transom. The materials given make a panel measuring 31 x 12in (79 x 30cm). Choose either the tulip or the onion pattern. (Cartoons on page 155).

*Glass*
Tulips: ¾sq ft (0.07sq m) red cathedral or opalescent
or Onions: ¼sq ft (0.025sq m) white and ¼sq ft (0.025sq m) purple
Leaves: 1sq ft (0.1sq m) green opalescent
Background: 1sq ft (0.1sq m) clear seedy or amber opalescent
Border: 1sq ft (0.1sq m) your choice

60/40 solder and flux
30ft (9m) H-channel lead (¼in)

Tulip and Onion panels

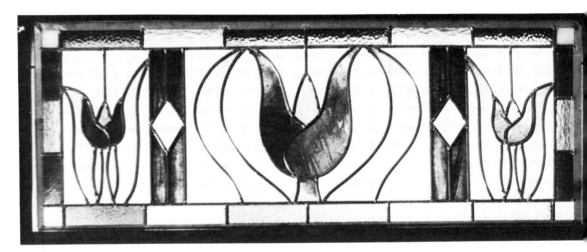

## Clown on Tightrope

*Project complexity: 9*
*Composed of 186 pieces of glass*

The materials given will make a panel
14 x 63in (35.5 x 160cm).

*Glass*
Pants and umbrella: 2sq ft (0.2sq m) yellow
 opalescent
Pants and umbrella: 2sq ft (0.2sq m) blue
 opalescent
Shirt: 1/4sq ft (0.025sq m) green opalescent
Shirt: 1/4sq ft (0.025 sq m) purple opalescent
Border: 1 1/2sq ft (0.14sq m) your choice
Face and glove: 1/3sq ft (0.031sq m) white
Hat, shoes, and tie: 1 1/2sq ft (0.14sq m) brown
Lips: 1/8sq ft (0.012sq m) red
Background: 2 1/2sq ft (0.25sq m) clear seedy
Sleeves: 1/2sq ft (0.05sq m) dark red
Hair: 3/4sq ft (0.07sq m) orange opalescent
Skin: 1/16sq ft (0.006sq m) amber
Bird: 1/8sq ft (0.012sq m) aqua
Braces (suspender) button: nugget or pearl
 button (1 1/2in or 38mm diameter)
Eye: glass eye or nugget
Nose: red nugget (1 1/2in or 38mm diameter)

60/40 solder and flux
62ft (19m) H-channel lead (1/4in)
13ft (4m) zinc (1/2in wide)

Fig 95  Clown on Tightrope (colour photograph
page 71)

## Harlequin

*Project complexity: 7*
*Assembly technique: foil*
*Composed of 83 pieces of glass*

The materials given will make a 12½ x 24in (32 x 61cm) panel.

*Glass*
Plain background: 10 x 12in (25 x 30cm) very light-blue or clear streaky cathedral.
Checked background: 6 x 10in (15 x 25cm) dark-blue cathedral
Checked background: 6 x 10in (15 x 25cm) milky white
Balls: 6 x 6in (15 x 15cm) yellow cathedral
Legs and arms: 12 x 12in (30 x 30cm) light streaky-blue cathedral
Cap, blouse, thighs: 12 x 14in (30 x 35.5cm) medium-blue cathedral
Face and neck: 6 x 12in (15 x 30cm) white opalescent
Lips: 1 x 2in (2.5 x 5cm) purple cathedral
Face streaks: 2 x 3in (5 x 7.5cm) orange cathedral

60/40 solder and flux
Foil (¼in)
74in (2m) U-channel zinc came (¼in)

The photograph of the panel (page 72) shows shadows on the chequered floor. These are not shown on the design, but can easily be drawn in if desired.

The nostrils are pieces of copper foil soldered in position over the glass and then covered with solder.

Fig 96   Harlequin (colour photograph page 72)

## Metamorphosis: Butterfly

*Project complexity: 6*
*Composed of 120 pieces of glass*

Metamorphosis is a set of three panels, one of which is 'Butterfly'. The other two, 'Caterpillar' and 'Cocoon', are illustrated overleaf. These materials will make a panel 26 x 36in (66 x 91.5cm).

*Glass*
Background: 6sq ft (0.55sq m) clear seedy
Wings: 2sq ft (0.2sq m) your choice
Leaves: ¼sq ft (0.025sq m) green opalescent
Body: ¼sq ft (0.025sq m) brown or purple
Border: 1sq ft (0.1 sq m) your choice

60/40 solder and flux
54ft (16.5m) H-channel lead (¼in)
11ft (3.5m) zinc (½in wide)
12in (30cm) U-channel lead (⅛in). This lead is tightly wound and tack soldered in position to form the butterfly's proboscis.

## Metamorphosis: Caterpillar

*Project complexity: 6*
*Composed of 140 pieces of glass*

These materials will make a panel 16 x 47in (40 x 119.5cm).

*Glass*
Leaves: 2sq ft (0.2sq m) light-green opalescent
Leaves: 1sq ft (0.1sq m) dark-green opalescent
Face: ⅛sq ft (0.012 sq m) purple
Body: 1 sq ft (0.1sq m) chartreuse
Stripes on body: ¼sq ft (0.025sq m) amber
Stem: ½sq ft (0.05sq m) brown
Border: 1sq ft (0.1sq m) your choice
Background: 4 sq ft (0.4sq m) clear seedy

60/40 solder and flux
55ft (17m) H-channel lead (¼in)
11ft (3.5m) zinc (½in wide)

## Metamorphosis: Cocoon

*Project complexity: 6*
*Composed of 160 pieces of glass*

These materials will make a panel 16 x 47in (40 x 119.5cm).

*Glass*
Leaves: 3sq ft (0.3sq m) green, different shades
Cocoon body: 1sq ft (0.1sq m) amber
Background: 4½sq ft (0.45sq m) clear seedy
Stem: ½sq ft (0.05sq m) brown
Flowers: ⅓sq ft (0.031sq m) red
Cocoon top: ⅛sq ft (0.012sq m) white
Border: 1sq ft (0.1sq m) your choice
Nuggets (¾in or 20mm), your choice

60/40 solder and flux
55ft (17m) H-channel lead (¼in)
11ft (3.5m) zinc (½in wide)

Fig 97   Metamorphosis: Butterfly (colour photograph page 98–9)

Fig 98  Metamorphosis: Caterpillar (colour photograph page 98–9)

Fig 99  Metamorphosis: Cocoon (colour photograph page 98–9)

160

## Janet

*Project complexity: 10*
*Assembly technique: must be leaded*
*Composed of 300 pieces of glass*

This panel can be a wall hanging with
mirror for the background, or a window
panel with clear seedy or amber opalescent for the background. Because the design is intricate and many of the pieces
are tiny, this design cannot be made
much smaller than the original 28 x 60in
(71 x 152.5cm). Enlarge the cartoon
using the grid method described in
Chapter 4.

*Glass*
Background: 7sq ft (0.65sq m) mirror, amber
   or seedy
Blouse: 1sq ft (0.1sq m) violet opalescent
Skirt: 1½sq ft (0.14 sq m) white
Hair: 1sq ft (0.1sq m) yellows
Birds: 1sq ft (0.1sq m) your choice
Leaves: 4 sq ft (0.4 sq m) green, different
   shades
Trellis: 2½sq ft (0.25sq m) white
Floor or ground: 1sq ft (0.1sq m) your choice

60/40 solder and flux
135ft (41m) H-channel lead (¼in)
15ft (4.5m) zinc (½in wide)

Fig 100   Janet (colour photograph page 97)

## Additional Panel Patterns

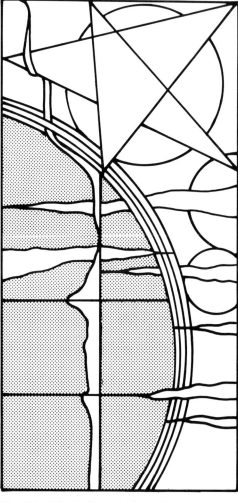

Fig 101  Tommy, a three-dimensional panel (colour photograph page 100). The fishing rod and line are a piece of bamboo and some string which extend out from the panel. The ends of the grass in Tommy's mouth are made of wire

Fig 102  Life in Space (colour photograph page 125). This design works well in porch or storm doors. The shaded areas are clear glass, allowing a view of outside

Fig 103  May Bouquet (colour photograph page
126)

Fig 104 Energy (colour photograph page 143). Various lenses were used in the original, some concave, others convex, for an unusual effect

Fig 106 Bouquet

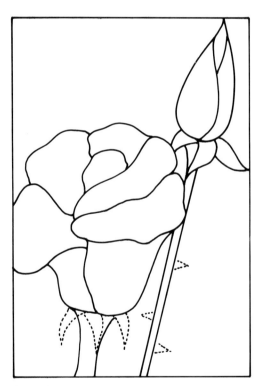

Fig 105 Rose and Bud. The thorns on the bud stem and the sepals at the base of the rose are made of copper foil covered with solder. Cover the copper before placing it on the glass, or the heat of the iron will crack the glass

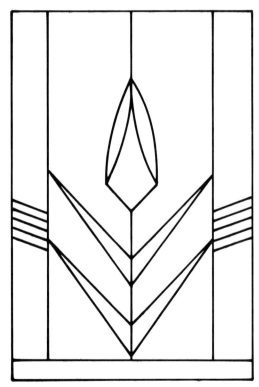

Fig 107 Untitled I

164

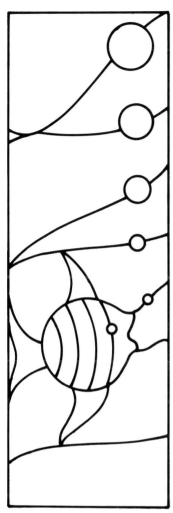

Fig 108 Bubbles. Use lenses, nuggets, or cut glass for the bubbles

Fig 109 Flower with Birds. Fill the centre of the flower with mirror or numerous amber nuggets (a few are shown)

Fig 110 Untitled II. This pattern can be used as shown, or the design above the dashed line can be turned over and drawn again to make a symmetrical design

165

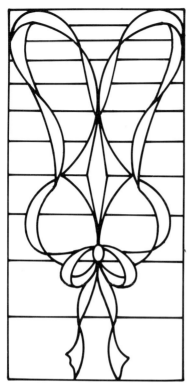

Fig 111   Ribbon with Diamond

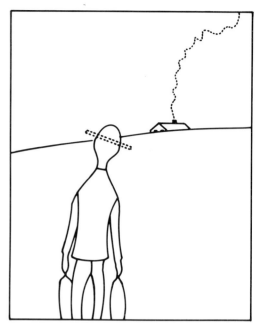

Fig 113   Where in the Hell is the Yellow Ribbon? (colour photograph page 144) For the smoke, wrap wire round a pencil, pull it into an irregular shape, then solder it to the chimney and panel edge. The hat brim is a strip of thin lead. The windows and chimney are tiny pieces of copper covered with solder. Make the silhouette from black opaque glass.

Use glass with an obvious pattern (see photograph) and keep the whole of the foreground, below the skyline, one continuous piece. Cut the figure out of this piece and discard the cut-out silhouette. Take care — if one piece of the background is broken, the whole background will have to be recut.

Fig 112 Peeper (colour photograph page 143). Paint the pupils or grind holes in the glass. The tuft of hair is copper foil covered with solder. The 'lady-bug' is a nugget and the antennae are wires with drops of solder on the end. Each lens is cut from nearly clear glass and soldered over the eyes. Wooden window partitions over the panel give it a three-dimensional effect (see photograph)

166

# Glossary

**Antique glass** Transparent hand-blown glass of varying thickness.

**Architectural glass** Stained-glass compositions designed for and permanently installed as a part of an architectural setting.

**Autonomous panel** A non-architectural stained-glass composition.

**Bead** A slightly raised line of solder along the junction between foiled pieces of glass.

**Bevelled glass** Thick glass (usually $3/16$-$1/4$in) with the surface near the edge inclined or slanted by a few to twenty degrees.

**Burnisher** A tool used to flatten and smooth copper foil against glass. A lathekin.

**Came** Strips of lead (or zinc), H-shaped or U-shaped in cross-section. Placed between pieces of glass in leaded panels.

**Cartoon** The drawing over which a stained-glass composition is constructed.

**Cathedral glass** A transparent machine-rolled glass usually $1/8$in thick.

**Cullet** Scrap glass.

**Cutter or glass cutter** Steel or carbide wheel on a handle used for scoring glass. Sometimes a diamond is used to scratch the glass.

**Etch** To erode the glass surface. To remove the thin layer of glass from flashed glass with hydrofluoric acid; or to produce a ground glass appearance on clear glass, usually in a decorative design with a commercially prepared etching paste or by sandblasting.

**Faceted window** A type of stained-glass window composed of thick chunks of glass (called slab glass) embedded in a cement or epoxy matrix. The glass edge is chipped with a hammer to produce irregular surfaces that refract light.

**Fid** A tool used to expand the groove in lead so glass will fit into it.

**Flashed glass** Antique glass composed of a thick base layer covered with a thin layer of a different colour. The flashed layer is removed by etching to create a design.

**Flux** A chemical used to prevent oxidation while soldering. Required for the adhesion of solder to lead, copper, or zinc.

**Foil** Copper ribbons of varying widths generally from $5/32$-$1/2$in with adhesive backing.

Placed around the edges of glass pieces and soldered to hold them together.

**Glaze** A term used in many ways but most commonly to put the glass pieces together to form a window or panel, and to install a window in an opening.

**Glob (nugget)** A small, round to oval, pre-formed, inexpensive piece of glass, flat on one side and curved on the other. Used in sun-catchers.

**Grozing** To nibble away irregular bits of glass from the edge of a piece of glass.

**Jewel** A small preformed piece of glass, flat on one side, smooth or faceted on the other. Better quality than globs.

**Lancet** A long narrow window that tapers to a Gothic arch at the top. Commonly found in churches.

**Lathekin (larupin)** A tool used to open lead channel to receive glass. Also used to flatten and smooth foil against glass.

**Leading** The method of joining pieces of glass together by securing the edges of the glass in the channel of lead strips, called came, which are then soldered at each point of intersection.

**Opalescent** Machine-rolled, translucent glass, usually with two or more colours.

**Patina** A chemical (usually copper-coloured or black) used to alter the colour and subdue the shine of solder.

**Pattern** A template, usually of thin cardboard, the exact shape of the piece of glass to be cut.

**Pattern shears** Special scissors used for cutting pattern pieces apart. Removes a sliver of paper from between the pattern pieces.

**Putty** Also called glazing compound. A substance used to seal a leaded panel. As a verb, it means to fill the space between the lead and glass with putty, an impervious material, and thereby strengthen and waterproof the panel.

**Rheostat** A device for regulating the amount of electrical current reaching the soldering iron, thereby controlling the temperature.

**Rondel** A disc of glass, usually with irregular or textured surfaces, used for special effects. The cut-off bottom of the cylinder formed in the process of making antique glass.

167

**Rose window** A circular window, usually with a pattern radiating from the centre.

**Score glass** To make a scratch mark on the surface of a piece of glass, usually with a rolling-wheel glass cutter.

**Seedy glass** Glass with tiny bubbles within it.

**SGAA** Stained Glass Association of America.

**Solder** A low-melting-point metal used to join copper or lead, composed of lead and tin. To solder is the act of applying solder.

**Stained glass** Glass embedded with metal oxides that produce colour.

**Suncatchers** Small glass trinkets made to hang in windows.

**Support rod (tie bar)** A horizontal bar affixed across large windows to prevent the glass from sagging and to strengthen the installation.

**Tack solder** Solder at strategic points to hold foiled pieces of glass in position during assembly.

**Translucent** Allows passage of light through glass but no image.

**Transparent** Glass through which an image can be seen.

**Zinc came** A came made of zinc that is used around the edge of panels to provide added strength and support.

# Suppliers

## UK

James Hetley & Co Ltd
Beresford Avenue
Wembley
Middlesex HA0 1RP
Tel: 01 903 4151
Glass, tools and all other supplies

Stained Glass Supplies
Unit 5
Brunel Way
Thornbury Industrial Estate
Thornbury
Avon
Tel: 0454 419975
Glass, tools and all other supplies

I.W.F. Ltd
27 Clayton Park Square
Newcastle Upon Tyne
NE2 4DP
Tel: 0632 812533
Tools

F. C. Randall & Son Ltd
726-732 Seven Sisters Road
London NI5 5NH
Tel: 01 800 4777
Glass

Louis Bennett & Co Ltd
361 Beverley Road
Hull HU5 1LA
Tel: 0482 42131
Glass

Caldermac Studios
126 Springfield Road
Belfast BT12 7DQ
Tel: 0232 42839
Glass

J. O. W. Haram Ltd
Shaw House
28 Rosyth Road
Glasgow G5 0YD
Tel: 041 429 7621
Glass

Pearson Glass Ltd
26 Dublin Street
Liverpool L3 7HH
Tel: 051 207 1474
Glass

Norman & Underwood (Glass) Ltd
11-27 Free School Lane
Leicester LE1 4FX
Tel: 0533 29781
Glass

R. M. Catterson-Smith Ltd
Tollesbury
Nr Maldon
Essex CM9 8SJ
Tel: 0621 869342
Kilns

## USA

S. A. Bendheim Co, Inc
122 Hudson Street
New York, New York 10013
Glass, tools, books, lead came, and general supplies

Delphi Art Associates
2224 E Michigan Avenue
Lansing, Michigan 48912
Grinders, tools, supplies, lead came, and patterns

Franklin Glass Studios
222 East Sycamore Street
Columbus, Ohio 43206
This firm is very good for hobbyists and small studios. Sells glass, supplies, tools, jewels, bevels, and books

Glassmaster's Guild
621 Avenue of Americas
New York, New York 10011
Books, glass, tools, and general supplies

Glastar Corporation
19515 Business Center Drive
Northridge, California 91324
Handles Glastar grinders, tools, and bevels

Kokomo Opalescent Glass Company
1310 South Market Street
Kokomo, Indiana 46901
Glass

Lamps Limited
PO Box 218
Lake Hiawatha, New Jersey 07034
Copper foil and lamp supplies

Lincoln Distributors
510 South 52nd Street # 104
Tempe, Arizona 85281
Glass, supplies, tools, books, patterns, and
lamp parts

C. and R. Loo, Inc
1550 62nd Street
Emeryville, California 94662
Tools, glass, jewels, and lead

Merry-Go-Round Glass
8010 Ball Road
Fort Smith, Arkansas 72903
Glass manufacturer

Nervo Distributors'
650 University Avenue
Berkeley, California 94710
Large supplier of tools, supplies, glass, and
books

Rainbow Art Glass Corp
49 Shark River Road
Neptune, New York 07753
Glass, supplies, tools, and kits

Royal Industrial Supply Company, Inc
7 Mothball Terrace
Passaic, New Jersey 07055
Good source of copper foil

Wensley Metal Products Company
1445 Osage Street
Denver, Colorado 80204
Good source of lead came

Whittemore and Durgin Glass Company
Box 2065
Hanover, Massachusetts 02339
Good catalogue. Large supplier of everything
needed for glass crafting

Paul Wissmach Glass Company, Inc
420 Stephens Street
Paden City, West Virginia 26159
Glass manufacturer

H. L. Worden Company
PO Box 519
Granger, Washington 98932
Large selection of lamp forms, lamp kits, and
jewels

# Bibliography

## UK

Douglas, Prof R W and Frank, Miss Susan, *A History of Glass Making* (G. T. Foulis & Co Ltd 1972)

Duncan, Alistair, *The Technique of Leaded Glass* (Batsford 1975)

Harrison, Martin, *Victorian Stained Glass* (Barrie & Jenkins 1980)

Lee, Lawrence, *Stained Glass Handbook for Artists* (Oxford University Press 1967)

Lee, Lawrence, *The Appreciation of Stained Glass* (Oxford University Press 1976)

Lee, Lawrence, Stephens, Francis and Seddon, George, *Stained Glass* (Mitchell Beazley 1976)

Piper, John, *Stained Glass Art or Anti-Art* (Studio Vista, Reinhold 1968)

Reynteins, Patrick, *The Technique of Stained Glass* (Batsford 1977)

Tysoe, Peter, *Glass Resin and Metal Construction* (Mills and Boon Ltd 1971)

Woodforde, Christopher, *English Stained and Painted Glass* (Oxford University Press 1954)

## USA

Isenberg, A. and S., *Crafting in Glass* (Chilton 1981)

Luciano, *Stained Glass Window Art* (Hidden House 1976)

Mollica, Peter, *Stained Glass Primer* (Mollica Press 1971)

O'Brien, Vincent, *Technique of Stained Glass* (Van Nostrand Reinhold 1977)

Wood, Paul, *Stained Glass Crafting* (Sterling 1971)

*Stained Glass,* the quarterly magazine of the Stained Glass Association of America, is also particularly helpful.

# Index